CONNECTICUT WALK BOOK©

SIXTEENTH EDITION

A complete guide
to major hiking trails
in Connecticut

Includes carefully detailed maps

Founded 1895

PUBLISHED BY

CONNECTICUT FOREST AND PARK
ASSOCIATION
INCORPORATED

16 MERIDEN ROAD, ROUTE 66, MIDDLEFIELD
MIDDLETOWN, CT 06457

ISBN 0-9619052-1-2
Publication No. 36-S

© Connecticut Forest and Park Association, Inc. 1990

CONNECTICUT BLUE-BLAZED HIKING TRAILS
ARE LOCATED ON PRIVATE, MUNICIPAL AND
STATE PROPERTY AND ARE USED
THROUGH THE COURTESY OF
THESE OWNERS AND AGENCIES.

**HIKERS SHOULD RESPECT THE PRIVILEGE
EXTENDED BY FOLLOWING THE
ESTABLISHED ROUTES.**

Hikers Use the Trails at Their Own Risk.

**CAMPING ALONG TRAILS AT
UNDESIGNATED PLACES IS PROHIBITED.**

Persons Using Blue-Blazed Hiking Trails

SHOULD

**RESPECT RARE PLANTS
DESTROY NO VEGETATION
CARRY OUT LITTER
LIGHT NO FIRES EXCEPT**
*Where Officially Designated
Fireplaces are Provided*

**TAKE ONLY PICTURES —
LEAVE ONLY FOOTPRINTS**

DUE TO CHANGES IN CONDITIONS, USE OF
THE INFORMATION IN THIS BOOK IS AT
THE SOLE RISK OF THE USER.

TABLE OF CONTENTS

	PAGE
TRAILS COMMITTEE	vii
TRAIL SECTION CHAIRS	vii
INTRODUCTION	xiii

GENERAL INFORMATION

LANDOWNER LIABILITY LAW	xvi
"RULES OF THE ROAD" FOR HIKERS	xviii
MAPS	xviii
EQUIPMENT NEEDED	xix
EMERGENCIES	xx
DISTRESS SIGNAL	xx
STATE PARKS AND FORESTS	xxi
CAMPING	xxi
YOUTH HOSTELS	xxi
NEW ENGLAND TRAIL CONFERENCE	xxi
APPALACHIAN MOUNTAIN CLUB	xxii
CONNECTICUT 400 CLUB	xxii
TRAIL GUIDE PUBLISHERS	xxiii
CFPA PUBLICATIONS	xxv
CONNECTICUT FOREST AND PARK ASSOCIATION	xxvi

HIKING TRAIL DESCRIPTIONS AND MAPS

AMERICAN LEGION AND PEOPLES FOREST TRAILS	2
MAP	121
APPALACHIAN TRAIL, CONNECTICUT	4
MAP	123

iii

CHATFIELD TRAIL	7
MAP	125
COCKAPONSET FOREST TRAILS	8
MAP	127
FALLS BROOK TRAIL	9
MAP	187
GAY CITY TRAILS	10
MAP	175
HOUSATONIC RANGE TRAIL	13
MAP	129
KETTLETOWN STATE PARK TRAILS	15
MAP	131
LILLINONAH TRAIL	16
MAP	133
MACEDONIA BROOK TRAILS	18
MAP	135
MACEDONIA RIDGE TRAIL	19
MAP	135
McLEAN GAME REFUGE TRAILS	21
MAP	137
MATTABESETT TRAIL	24
MAP #1	139
MAP #2	143
MATTATUCK TRAIL	32
MAP	141
METACOMET TRAIL	36
MAP, RT. 15 TO U.S. 6	143
MAP, U.S. 6 TO TARIFFVILLE	145
MAP, NORTH SECTION	147
MOHAWK TRAIL	42
MAP	123
MUIR TRAIL	45
MAP	149
NARRAGANSETT TRAIL	45
MAP	165
NATCHAUG TRAIL	48
MAP #1	151
MAP #2	153

NAUGATUCK TRAIL	51
MAP	183
NAYANTAQUIT TRAIL	51
MAP	155
NEHANTIC TRAIL	53
MAP	163
NIPMUCK TRAIL	54
MAP #1	157
MAP #2	159
OLD FURNACE TRAIL	64
MAP	161
PACHAUG TRAIL	64
MAP	163
PAUGUSSETT TRAIL	71
MAP	131
PEQUOT TRAIL	73
MAP	165
PINE KNOB LOOP TRAIL	74
MAP	167
QUINEBAUG TRAIL	75
MAP	169
QUINNIPIAC TRAIL	76
MAP	183
RAGGED MOUNTAIN PRESERVE TRAIL	78
MAP	143
REGICIDES TRAIL	79
MAP	183
SALMON RIVER TRAIL	80
MAP	171
SHENIPSIT TRAIL	82
MAP #1	173
MAP #2	175
MAP #4	177
SLEEPING GIANT TRAILS	88
MAP	179
SUNNY VALLEY FOUNDATION TRAILS	92
MAP	181

TUNXIS TRAIL	93
MAP, SOUTH OF U.S. 44	185
MAP, NORTH OF U.S. 44	187
WATERBURY AREA TRAILS	114
MAP	141
WESTWOODS AND STONY CREEK	
QUARRY PRESERVE TRAILS	115
MAP	189
MAP, SOUTHERN SECTION	191
ZOAR TRAIL	116
MAP	131

OTHER TRAILS

	TEXT	MAP
BOWEN (AGNES) TRAIL	3	121
BRONSON (ELLIOTT) TRAIL	3	121
BUCK (HENRY) TRAIL	2	121
CANONICUS TRAIL	67	163
COMPOUNCE CASCADES TRAIL	98	185
CREST TRAIL	16	131
GIRARD (JESSIE) TRAIL	3	121
HANCOCK BROOK —		
LION HEAD TRAIL	114	141
JERICHO TRAIL	114	141
MILLER TRAIL	16	131
OLD FOREST TRAIL	9	127
PACK (CHARLES) TRAIL	3	121
PATACONK TRAIL	9	127
PHARISEE ROCK TRAIL	68	169
POMPERAUG TRAIL	15	131
ROSS (ROBERT) TRAIL	3	121
SEVEN FALLS LOOP	25	139
TIPPING ROCK LOOP	111	185
VALLEY OUTLOOK TRAIL	112	185
WHITESTONE CLIFFS TRAIL	114	141
WILDWOOD TRAIL	9	127

TRAILS COMMITTEE

CLYDE S. BROOKS, CHAIRMAN	Glastonbury
RICHARD BLAKE	Milford
DAN CASEY	Bristol
DOUGLAS CHRISTIE	West Hartford
NEIL CLARK	New Britain
SAMUEL G. DODD	Mansfield Center
EDGAR DRESNER	Vernon
DALE HACKETT	West Hartford
GRIFFITH JUNE	Guilford
GARY LEAVITT	New Milford
DANE P. MILLETTE	Cromwell
JOHN RANDALL	East Lyme
SEYMOUR R. SMITH	Watertown
A. RAYMOND TABERMAN	Waterford
JOHN E. HIBBARD, SECRETARY	Hebron

TRAIL SECTION CHAIRS

AMERICAN LEGION and PEOPLES STATE FOREST, Walter F. Landgraf, P.O. Box 88, Pleasant Valley 06063

APPALACHIAN, Appalachian Mountain Club, Connecticut Chapter, Glenn Parchmann, 75 Ridgewood Dr., Rocky Hill 06067

CHATFIELD, Donald Merry, 10 Papermill Road, Killingworth 06417

COCKAPONSET FOREST, Griffith L. June, 3832 Durham Road, Guilford 06437

FALLS BROOK, Emerson Harrison, 38 Sunny Slope Dr., Glastonbury 06033

GAY CITY STATE PARK, Richard Whitehouse, 1543 Manchester Rd., Glastonbury 06033

HOUSATONIC RANGE, New Milford Youth Agency, Gary Leavitt, 50 East St., New Milford 06776

KETTLETOWN STATE PARK (Miller, Crest & Pomperaug), Allen Crepeau, 113 Burr Rd., Southbury 06488

LILLINONAH, Chuck MacMath, 12 Shelbourne Rd., Trumbull 06611

MACEDONIA BROOK STATE PARK, Western District, Department of Environmental Protection, RFD 4, Plymouth Rd., Harwinton 06791

MACEDONIA RIDGE TRAIL, Norman Sills, Taconic Rd., Salisbury 06068

MATTABESETT, Connecticut River to Brooks Rd., John LeShane, South Rd., Portland 06480

MATTABESETT, Brooks Rd. to Rt. 154, Dane P. Millette, 2 Nordland Ave., Cromwell 06416-2320

MATTABESETT, Rt. 154 to Rt. 79, Bill Engstrom, 43 Newton Rd., Branford 06405

MATTABESETT, Rt. 79 to Rt. 17, Edward E. Merry, 49 Killingworth Tnpke., Clinton 06413

MATTABESETT, Rt. 17 to Rt. 66, Green Mountain Club, Connecticut Chapter, Richard Krompegal, 142 Church Dr., Newington 06111

MATTABESETT, Rt. 66 to Rt. 15, Connecticut Women Outdoors, Deborah Johnson, 217 Dunham St., #1, Southington 06489

MATTATUCK, Mad River Rd. to Rt. 8, Michael J. Heller, 9 Resevoir Rd., Newtown, CT 06470

MATTATUCK, Rt. 8 to Rt. 109, Elizabeth Buckley, 590 Amity Rd., Woodbridge 06525

MATTATUCK, Rt. 109 to Maple St., Terry Lincoln, 233 Redstone Hill Rd. Apt. A-6, Bristol 06010

MATTATUCK, North Rd. to Prospect Mountain Rd., Ken Nolan, P.O. Box 192, Bantam 06750

MATTATUCK, Milton to Mohawk Mountain, Ron Naylor, 246 Harwinton Ave., Torrington 06790

McLEAN GAME REFUGE, Steven A. Paine, 150 Barndoor Hills Rd., Granby 06035

METACOMET, Rt. 15 to Rt. 364, Gardner W. Moulton, 487 Fountain St., New Haven 06515-1830

METACOMET, Rt. 364 to Rt. 6, Joseph Ohara, 400 Church St., Wethersfield 06109

METACOMET, Rt. 6 to Rt. 185, Edward P. Regan, 10 Bramley Rd., West Hartford 06110

METACOMET, Rt. 185 to Tariffville, Dale Hackett, 28 Whitman Ave., West Hartford 06107

METACOMET, Tariffville to Massachusetts State Line, A. Raymond Taberman, 9 Raymond Ln. Waterford 06385

MOHAWK, Cornwall Bridge to Valley Rd., Neil Clark, 51 Westwood Drive, New Britain 06052

MOHAWK, Valley Rd. to Rt. 4, Colin Tait, 290 Litchfield Rd., Norfolk 06058

MOHAWK, Rt. 4 to Lake Rd., Bob Sprong, 50 Forest Rd., Newington 06111

MOHAWK, Lake Rd. to Mansfield Rd., Paul Hermenau, 1143 Marshall Lake Rd., Torrington 06790

MOHAWK, Mansfield Rd. to Dean's Ravine, Maria Mendes, 1642 New Haven Ave., Milford 06460

MOHAWK, Dean's Ravine to Falls Village, Forman School Outing Club, Deb McGinley, The Forman School, Litchfield 06759

MUIR, JOHN, Jay Bacca, 269 Edgewood Dr., Torrington 06790

NARRAGANSETT, Bill Ofsiany, Disaray Hill RFD#1, Norwich 06360

NATCHAUG, Rt. 6 to Rt. 198, Charles Rose, 117 Cooper St., Manchester 06040

NATCHAUG, Rt. 198 to Westford, Robert Schoff, RFD#3, Stafford Springs 06076

NAUGATUCK, Paul Pikula, 53 Summerfield St., Naugatuck 06770

NAYANTAQUIT, Nehantic State Forest, James S. Wheeler, 51 Black Point Rd., Niantic 06357

NEHANTIC, Green Fall Pond to Mt. Misery, Timothy L. Tallman, 23 Bozrah Dr., Norwich 06360

NEHANTIC, Mt. Misery to Hopeville Pond, Duncan I. Bailey, 26 Reservoir Rd., Norwich 06360

NIPMUCK, South, Samuel G. Dodd, 86 Puddin' Ln., Mansfield Center 06250

NIPMUCK, Marsh Rd. to Westford-Eastford Rd. (Ashford), David Raczkowski, 234 Singleton Rd., Chaplin 06235

NIPMUCK, Westford-Eastford Rd. to Rt. 171 (Union), Robert Mancini, 60 Kinney Hollow Rd., Union, Stafford Springs 06076

NIPMUCK, Rt. 171 to Massachusetts State Line, Edgar Dresner, 183 Hany Ln., Vernon 06066

OLD FURNACE STATE PARK, Richard J. Benoit, 490 Main St., Norwich 06360

PACHAUG, Green Fall Pond to Beach Pond, Gaboury Benoit & d'Ann de Simone, 162 Beach St., Westerly, RI 02891

PACHAUG, Beach Pond to Porter Rd. Pequotsepos Outing Club, Philip E. Rusch, 29-4 Nollett Rd., Mansfield Center 06250

PACHAUG, Porter Rd. to Hell Hollow Rd., John Randall, 12 Overbrook Rd., East Lyme 06333

PACHAUG, Hell Hollow Rd. to Rt. 138, Don Fortunato, P.O. Box 368, East Lyme 06333

PAUGUSSETT, Richard Blake, 11 Argyle Rd., Milford 06460

PEQUOT, Dave McClary, 93 Jeremy Hill Rd., North Stonington 06359

PINE KNOB, Appalachian Mountain Club, Connecticut Chapter, Norman Sills, Taconic Rd., Salisbury 06068

POMPERAUG, Allen Crempau, 113 Burr Rd., Southbury 06488

QUINEBAUG, Ken Nash, 17 Mohunganuck Trail, Voluntown 06384

QUINNIPIAC, Banton St. to Old Hartford Tnpke., North Haven Land Trust, David Holstein, 59 Laydon Ave., North Haven 06473

QUINNIPIAC, Old Hartford Tnpke. to Whitney Ave., Sleeping Giant Park Assoc., John Menta, 2A Dogwood Hill Rd., Hamden 06518

QUINNIPIAC, Whitney Ave. to Gaylord Mt. Rd., New Haven Hiking Club, Ron Letsch, 105 Hillside Ave., Shelton 06484

QUINNIPIAC, Gaylord Mt. Rd. to Rt. 42, Kathy Gentile, 29 Hilltop Rd., Hamden 06514

QUINNIPIAC, Rt. 42 to Rt. 68, William Schumacher, 184 Howe Ave., Shelton 06484

RAGGED MOUNTAIN MEMORIAL PRESERVE, Dale O. Hackett, 28 Whitman Ave., West Hartford 06107

REGICIDES, West Rock Ridge Park Association, Dr. William Doheny, Jr., 220 Mountain Rd., Hamden 06517

SALMON RIVER TRAIL, Clyde S. Brooks, 41 Baldwin Ln., Glastonbury 06033

SHENIPSIT, Great Hill to Rt. 94, Clyde S. Brooks, 41 Baldwin Ln., Glastonbury 06033

SHENIPSIT, Rt. 94 to I-384, Richard Whitehouse, 1543 Manchester Rd., Glastonbury 06033

SHENIPSIT, I-86 to Massachusetts State Line, John A. Guros, 37 Play Rd., Enfield 06082

SLEEPING GIANT STATE PARK, Sleeping Giant Park Association, John Menta, 2A Dogwood Hill Rd., Hamden 06518

SUNNY VALLEY FOUNDATION TRAILS, Sunny Valley Foundation, Dr. Stephen Kaffka, 4 Sunny Valley Ln., New Milford 06776

TUNXIS, South of Satan's Kingdom, Dan Casey, 49 Seymour St., Bristol 06010

TUNXIS, Rt. 44 to Ski Sundown, John S. Graecen, 16 Reverknolls, Avon 06001

TUNXIS, Ski Sundown to Rt. 219, Ben Warner, Warner Rd., Barkhamsted, RFD, Collinsville 06022

TUNXIS, Rt. 219 to Rt. 20, Lee Fielden, RFD, Collinsville 06022

TUNXIS, Rt. 20 to Massachusetts State Line, Kent Heidenis, 2 Volovski Rd., Avon 06001

WATERBURY AREA TRAILS, James Miller, 12 Raymond St., Waterbury 06706

WESTWOODS TRAILS, Guilford Land Conservation Trust, Kirt Griffin, 638 West Lake Ave., Guilford 06437

ZOAR, Richard Blake, 11 Argyle Rd., Milford 06460

INTRODUCTION

Where shall we walk today? This book was compiled to help you find the answer. Connecticut, with its rugged hills, trap rock ridges, and gently rolling country, provides excellent hiking. Although the state is densely populated, there is a surprising amount of attractive and accessible wild land. Go out for a few miles from your home, and you can soon be on a forest trail. You can drive to a distant part of the state, put in a day of good hiking, and be back in your own bed at night.

Since 1929 the Trails Committee of the Connecticut Forest and Park Association and its trail section chairs have been laying out and maintaining hiking trails. The first edition of the CONNECTICUT WALK BOOK appeared in 1937. Subsequent editions have reflected gradual expansion of the trail system and the many changes in trail routes necessitated by changes in land use. The trail descriptions and maps have been revised for the sixteenth edition to match changes in the trails, as reported by the trail section chairs. In addition, two new trails are included — the John Muir Trail in Torrington and a section of The Appalachian Trail relocated to go through Sharon west of the Housatonic River. Also the section of the A. T. replaced by the relocation has been retained as a blue-blazed trail, designated the Mohawk Trail.

The trail descriptions in general are written for travel from S to N. Exceptions are noted. Only marked trails are described, unless a wood road provides a convenient connection to a highway, trail or the starting point. At the beginning of all trail sections reference is made to the U.S.G.S. topographic quadrangle(s) covering that region.

Credit should be given to our volunteer trail crews — busy men and women who work on trails in spare hours and provide their own tools and gasoline. The Association stresses that trails are maintained by *volunteers*. Hikers can provide valuable assistance by removing branches, obstructions (except where placed to discourage off-road vehicles), and litter from the trail.

Except for the Appalachian Trail, which is marked by white blazes, and certain state park and side trails, marked by blazes in a variety of colors, the trails of the Connecticut system are marked in light blue in the form of blazes, arrows, or targets. Unless otherwise indicated, all the walks described herein are so marked. Cutover land and pastures are hard to mark; in such places, look for blue targets at a distance, rock cairns, rags on bushes, or traces of cuttings. Oval trail signs can be found at some state highway crossings.

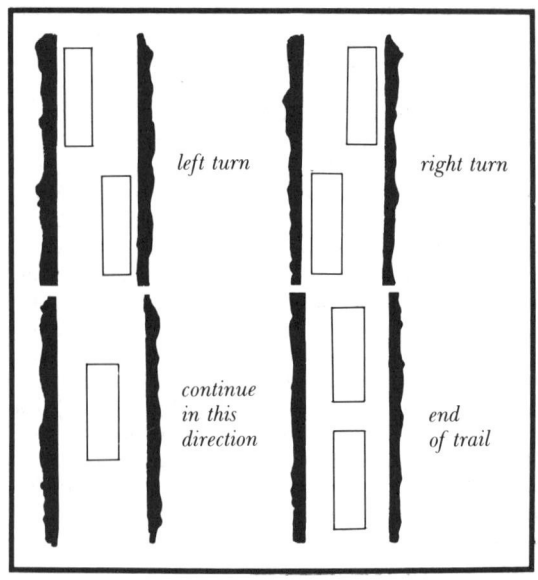

The Four Standard Blaze Arrangements

The names and addresses of the trail section chairs are given on p. vii. They may be consulted for information about changes in trail routes. The Association welcomes comments and suggestions from hikers — particularly reports regarding stretches of trail where the marking or brushing requires attention or where the trail route has been interrupted.

Hikers travel at their own risk. Public Act 249 of the 1971 General Assembly limits the liability of property owners of land used for recreational purposes. The law provides that persons using land for recreational purposes are not relieved of any obligation to exercise care in their use of the land. The law has been upheld by Connecticut courts.

The use of Blue-Blazed Hiking Trails located

on private land by motorized vehicles, such as snowmobiles, motorcycles, and off-road vehicles (ORVs), is prohibited. The Association would like information about instances of any unauthorized use of trails.

Fires must not be lit except where OFFICIALLY designated fireplaces have been provided. Hikers should be particularly careful with matches, pipe heels, and cigarette stubs. Severe penalties are imposed by law for setting fires intentionally or by carelessness.

Except on state land, which is open to the public for proper use, our trails exist only by courtesy of the landowners. Hikers must follow the route indicated and not roam through the property at will. Hikers should constitute themselves a voluntary patrol to see that the "Rules of the Road for Hikers", given on p. xviii, are followed. Carelessness on a hiker's part may cause a trail to be abandoned.

The present guide book is intended for hikers rather than strollers. Although the walks described are of moderate length, they are often steep and rough and should not be attempted without proper footwear. Suggestions about equipment for hikes are given on p. xix.

A new form of protection for some of the blue-blazed trails that traverse land under the control of the Department of Environmental Protection was proposed in December 1989. Sections of a number of trails were nominated for the designation of "Scenic Hiking Trails," which would then be subject to certain restrictions with respect to timber harvesting and related activities. If the DEP decides to adopt this recommendation, the "Scenic Hiking Trails" will be announced in *"Connecticut Woodlands"* and then will be listed in the next edition of *The Walk Book*.

The WALK BOOK is the official hiking guide to the Connecticut system of Blue Trails. Many persons have worked on this edition, including, of course, all of our trail section chairs.

The information contained in the publication was current at the time it was submitted. However, we cannot guarantee its accuracy at any point in time.

We wish the reader many happy hours exploring Connecticut trails.

JOHN S. BURLEW
Editor

GENERAL INFORMATION

LANDOWNER LIABILITY LAW

Connecticut General Statutes as amended

Sec. 52-557f. Definitions. As used in sections 52-557f to 52-557i, inclusive: (a) "Land" means land, roads, water, watercourses, private ways and buildings, structures, and machinery or equipment when attached to the realty; (b) "owner" means the possessor of a fee interest, a tenant, lessee, occupant or person in control of the premises; (c) "recreational purpose" includes, but is not limited to, any of the following, or any combination thereof: Hunting, fishing, swimming, boating, camping, picnicking, hiking, pleasure driving, nature study, water skiing, snow skiing, ice skating, sledding and viewing or enjoying historical, archaeological, scenic or scientific sites, or cutting and removing wood: (d) "charge" means the admission price or fee asked in return for invitation or permission to enter or go upon the land.

Sec. 52-557g. Owner of land available to public for recreation not liable, when. (a) Except as provided in section 52-557h, an owner of land who makes all or any part of such land available to the public without charge, rent, fee or other commercial service for recreational purposes owes no duty of care to keep such land or the part thereof so made available safe for entry or use by others for recreational purposes, or to give any warning of a dangerous condition, use, structure or activity on such premises to persons entering for such purposes.

(b) Except as provided in section 52-577h, an owner of land who, either directly or indirectly, invites or permits without charge, rent, fee or other commercial service any person to use such land or part thereof for recreational purposes does not thereby: (1) Make any representation that the premises are safe for any purpose; (2) confer upon such person who enters or uses such land for such recreational purposes the legal status of an invitee or licensee to whom a duty of care is owed; (3) assume responsibility for or incur liability for any injury to person or property caused by an act or omission of such owner.

(c) Unless otherwise agreed in writing, the provisions of subsection (a) and (b) of this section shall be deemed applicable to the duties and liability of an owner of land leased to the state or any subdivision thereof for recreational purposes.

Sec. 52-557h. Owner liable, when. Nothing in sections 52-557f to 52-557i, inclusive, limits in any way the liability of any owner of land which otherwise exists: (a) For willful or malicious failure to guard or warn against a dangerous condition, use, structure or activity; (b) for injury suffered in any case where the owner of land charges the person or persons who enter or go on the land for the recreational use thereof, except that, in the case of land leased to the state or a subdivision thereof, any consideration received by the owner for such lease shall not be deemed a charge within the meaning of this section.

Sec. 52-557i. Obligation of user of land. Nothing in sections 52-557f to 52-557i, inclusive, shall be construed to relieve any person using the land of another for recreational purposes from any obligation which he may have in the absence of said sections to exercise care in his use of such land and in his activities thereon, or from the legal consequences of failure to employ such care.

Sec. 52-557j. Liability of landowner upon whose land snowmobiles, all terrain vehicles, motorcycles, mini-bikes or minicycles are operated. No landowner shall be liable for any injury sustained by any person operating a snowmobile, all terrain vehicle, as defined in section 14-379, motorcycle or a mini-bike or mini-cycle, as defined in section 14-1, upon such landowner's property or by any passenger in such snowmobile, all terrain vehicle or motorcycle, mini-bike or mini-cycle, whether or not such landowner had given permission, written or oral, for such operation upon his land unless such landowner charged a fee for such operation, or unless such injury is caused by the willful or malicious conduct of such landowner.

"RULES OF THE ROAD" FOR HIKERS

Approved by the Connecticut Forest and Park Association

While Camping

1. Camp only in designated areas.
2. Be careful with fires; make them only in specified sites; put them out completely before leaving them.
3. "Carry In — Carry Out" — everything.

On the Trail

1. Stay on the right of way.
2. Leave all flowers, mushrooms, wildlife, rocks, etc., for the next hiker to enjoy.
3. Respect peace and quiet on the trails.
4. Leave all gates and barways as you found them.
5. When hiking with your dog, keep your dog under control at all times.
6. Pick up litter you find on the trail.
7. Be friendly with those you meet on the trail.
8. Give horseback riders the right of way.
9. Report any dangerous trail conditions to the proper authority: The Connecticut Forest and Park Association, 16 Meriden Rd., Middletown, CT 06457, Tel 346-2372, will forward the information to the party responsible for the trail.

General

1. Be considerate of the landowner's wishes.
2. Obey all signs, especially "No Trespassing".
3. "Be Prepared" — carry adequate equipment suitable for your trip. See section below: "Equipment Needed".
4. Before hiking in Connecticut, get a copy of the Connecticut Forest and Park Association's *Connecticut Walk Book* for detailed trail information.

MAPS

The Connecticut Forest And Park Association does not sell individual hiking trail maps. Trail maps are included in the *Connecticut Walk Book*.

The State of Connecticut annually publishes a

map of the state showing highways and outdoor recreational facilities such as state parks, state forests, and major hiking trails. It is available free from the Department of Environmental Protection, Information and Education Unit; mailing address: 165 Capitol Ave., Hartford, CT 06106; Department of Transportation, Bureau of Highways, mailing address: P.O. Drawer A, Wethersfield, CT 06109; Department of Economic Development, 865 Brook Street, Rocky Hill, CT 06067.

Topographic maps on the scale of 1 inch = 2000 ft., covering the entire area of the state, are obtainable from the U.S. Geological Survey, Washington, D.C. 20242. These maps are also obtainable from the Natural Resources Center, Information and Education Unit, Department of Environmental Protection, Hartford 06106 at $3.00 each plus tax. They are also sold by Clapp and Treat, Inc., 674 Farmington Ave., West Hartford, CT 06119; Eastern Mountain Sports, 1 Civic Center Plaza, Hartford, CT 06103; Whitlock's Inc., 15 Broadway, New Haven, CT 06511; and other firms.

EQUIPMENT NEEDED

On Connecticut trails, use sturdy hiking shoes with broad toes. Allow plenty of room for one or two pairs of wool socks, which make good padding. To rest the feet, turn the socks inside out or interchange rights and lefts, if possible hanging in the air for a few minutes. Shoes should be kept pliable with a good leather oil or grease, which also makes them more water-repellent. Always break in new shoes before using them on a long hike.

For clothing, we recommend flannel shirts, light woolen underwear to prevent chilling, loose-fitting khaki pants, a light-weight sweater for extra warmth, and as protection against wind and rain either a windbreaker or parka. It is wise to carry an extra pair of socks.

A light knapsack should be used for lunch, extra clothing, etc. It is important to carry a container of water or a thermos with a hot beverage. In addition, hikers in need of water should obtain it at public places rather than requesting homeowners along trails for water. Some of the streams which one crosses are safe for drinking, but as a precaution in case of doubt take along some chlorine tablets. (Add one to a quart of water, and aerate). Sun glasses will prevent eyestrain. It is always wise to carry a knife of some sort, a first aid kit, and a flashlight.

If you lose the trail, follow the next brook or wood road down to a road. A compass is useful.

EMERGENCIES

A simple first-aid kit will take care of ordinary scratches or cuts. For protection against mosquitoes or black flies many repellents are available. Poison Ivy and insect stings can be alleviated with First Aid Cream or other such preparations.

For dislocations or sprains, apply cold water and devise a sling. For bone fractures, cut away clothing, and make a splint, keeping the broken ends of the bone slightly separated; carry the injured to the nearest highway on a stretcher made of two poles run through the alternate sleeve holes of two coats or sweaters; or form a cradle with locked hands, the injured person putting his arm around the neck of the carriers. Get prompt medical attention.

Though rattlesnakes and copperheads are not common, they are found on the trails. If bitten, avoid excitement above all things. Take the patient as quietly as possible to the nearest highway and call a doctor or hospital. Snakebite serum can be brought to any part of Connecticut in time to avoid serious consequences. A venom extractor kit may be carried.

DISTRESS SIGNAL

The uniform distress signal in the woods, adopted by the American Alpine Club and approved by our Trails Committee, is a sequence of three quickly repeated signals (audible or visual) repeated at regular intervals. One may shout, fire a pistol, blow a whistle, flash a light, disclose a fire or smudge, or wave something, *three* times quickly. Repeat the signal regularly. This signal should be used only in case of actual distress.

Any hiker receiving a distress signal is morally bound to go to the rescue; the answer is *two* signals repeated at intervals.

STATE PARKS AND FORESTS

The Department of Environmental Protection through its Office of State Parks and Recreation has developed many recreational areas, with facilities for camping, picnicking, swimming and hiking. Some of the blue-blazed trails cross Connecticut's state forests and state parks. In addition there are many miles of both marked and unmarked trails and wood roads for exploration and enjoyment.

CAMPING

Camping along the trails at undesignated places is *prohibited*. Increased vandalism in recent years has reinforced the necessity of this policy.

Camping is permitted in several of the state parks. For camping arrangements, write the Bureau of Parks and Forests, Department of Environmental Protection, 165 Capitol Ave., Hartford, CT 06106.

In the state forests there are a few open shelters, with fireplaces.

YOUTH HOSTELS

Yankee Council American Youth Hostels offers recreational bicycling, hiking, and canoeing trips, organized by trained leaders. AYH has hostels at Bantam Lake, Bolton and Windsor. Contact Yankee Council A.Y.H., 118 Oak Street, Hartford, CT 06106, Tel. 247-6356.

NEW ENGLAND TRAIL CONFERENCE

The Conference is a federation of about 50 organizations in New England interested in hiking and bridle trails and serves as a general clearing house and promotion agency. For general information on New England trails, address Forrest E. House, N.E.T.C., 33 Knollwood Drive, East Longmeadow, MA 01028.

APPALACHIAN MOUNTAIN CLUB

The Appalachian Mountain Club with headquarters at 5 Joy St., Boston, MA 02108 was organized in 1876. It publishes a monthly bulletin, a semi-annual periodical, *Appalachia*, and many trail guides. The Connecticut Chapter carries out a program of the Connecticut section hikes throughout the year. The chapter maintains 51 miles of the Appalachian Trail and has taken an active interest in other trail development. Our Trails Committee and many of our trail maintainers are largely recruited from its ranks.

CONNECTICUT 400 CLUB

A "Connecticut 400" award was established by the Connecticut Chapter of the Appalachian Mountain Club in 1976 as recognition of those whose enjoyment of hiking has led them to hike all the major trails of Connecticut. One of the aims of the award is to encourage people to use all the trails available to them in the State.

To qualify, an individual must hike all of the trails and side loops as listed below.

Trail	Date Started	Date Completed	Trail	Date Started	Date Completed
American Legion			Nehantic		
Appalachian			Nipmuck		
Canonicus			Pachaug		
Chatfield			Pequot		
Cockaponset			Pomperaug		
Falls Brook			Quinnebaug		
Gay City			Quinnipiac		
Housatonic			Ragged Mountain		
Macedonia Brook			Regicides		
McClean Game Refuge			Salmon River		
Mattabesett			Shenipsit		
Mattatuck			Sleeping Giant		
Metacomet			Stony Creek Quarry		
Narragansett			Sunny Valley		

Trail	Date Started	Date Completed	Trail	Date Started	Date Completed
Natchaug			Tunxis		
Naugatuck			Waterbury Area		
Nayantaquit			Westwoods		

For further information send a self-addressed stamped envelope to Dr. Daryll C. Borst, Dept. of Biological Sciences, Quinnipiac College, Hamden, CT 06518.

TRAIL GUIDE PUBLISHERS

The Adirondack Mountain Club, Inc.
R.R. 3, Box 3055
Lake George, NY 12845
　Adirondack Sampler, Day Hikes
　Adirondack Sampler II, Backpacking
　Guide to Adirondack Trails: High Peaks Region
　Guide to Adirondack Trails: Northern Region
　Guide to Adirondack Trails: Central Region
　Guide to the Northville — Placid Trail
　Guide to Adirondack Trails: West-Central Region
　Guide to Adirondack Trails: Eastern Region
　Guide to Adirondack Trails: Southern Region
　Guide to Catskill Trails

Appalachian Mountain Club
5 Joy St.
Boston, MA 02108
(Also sells other N.E. Trail Guides.)
　AMC Maine Mountain Guide
　AMC Massachusetts and Rhode Island Trail Guide
　AMC White Mountain Guide

Appalachian Trail Conference
Box 807
Harpers Ferry, WV 25425
　Appalachian Trail Guide to Massachusetts — Connecticut
　Appalachian Trail Guide to New Hampshire — Vermont
　Appalachian Trail Guide to Maine

The Countryman Press
Backcountry Publications
Box 175
Woodstock, VT 05091

50 Hikes in Connecticut, 3rd Ed. (Available 1991) by Sue and Gerry Hardy
Walks and Rambles in Westchester and Fairfield Counties (updated 1988), by Katherine S. Anderson

The Globe Pequot Press, Inc.
Box Q
Chester, CT 06412
Sixty Selected Short Walks in Connecticut
A Guide to New England's Landscape
Short Bike Rides in Connecticut
Best Bike Rides in New England
Cross Country Skiing in New England (2nd ed.)

Green Mountain Club
P.O. Box 889
Montpelier, VT 05601
Day Hikers Guide to Vermont
Guide Book to the Long Trail
Mt. Mansfield Trail Map
Camel's Hump Trail Map
End to End Topographical Map Set

The Nature Conservancy, Connecticut Chapter
55 High St.
Middletown, CT 06457
Country Walks in Connecticut: A Guide to the Nature Conservancy Preserves by Susan D. Cooley

New England Trail Conference
Forrest E. House
33 Knollwood Dr.
East Longmeadow, MA 01028
Map, Hiking Trails of New England
Annual Report, New England Trails

Sleeping Giant Park Association
Box 14, Quinnipiac College
Hamden, CT 06518
Map of Trails in Sleeping Giant State Park
Large map available from Park Manager.
Membership information available from above address.

NOTE: Prior to placing orders, persons should request current prices from the publisher.

Founded 1895

CFPA Publications

Connecticut Walk Book, $14 per copy plus $3 for sales tax, postage, and handling.

Forest Trees of Southern New England tree manual, a tree identification handbook which describes the forest trees common to this region. It gives the names and descriptions of forty-eight forest trees with black line illustrations of their leaves and twigs. Also, simple identification keys for summer and winter are included. Woodland owners, hikers and all persons interested in our forest trees should find the manual of considerable value. Pages are provided for recording where and when particular trees are first identified, as well as for other field notes.

Price per copy is $1.00 plus $1.00 to cover sales tax, postage, and handling. Twenty-five or more copies to one address for $.80 each.

Checks payable to Connecticut Forest and Park Association. Send orders to Connecticut Forest and Park Association, 16 Meriden Rd., Middletown, CT 06457. Pre-payment required.

CONNECTICUT FOREST AND PARK ASSOCIATION

The Connecticut Forest And Park Association, organized in 1895, is a general clearing house for outdoor interests in Connecticut. It has been active in promoting state parks and forests, scientific forestry and markets for forest products, roadside improvement, and facilities for outdoor recreation.

The Association is a voluntary agency, *having no official connection with the state,* and is supported by dues and contributions. The Association magazine, *Connecticut Woodlands,* issued four times a year, keeps the members in touch with new developments and publications in hiking and various phases of forestry and conservation.

Questions on outdoor recreation in Connecticut and elsewhere may be sent to the office, Connecticut Forest and Park Association, 16 Meriden Rd., Middletown, CT 06457, telephone 346-2372.

....

MEMBERSHIP APPLICATION

MEMBERSHIP CATEGORIES

- ☐ Individual $25
- ☐ Family $45
- ☐ Student $15
- ☐ Sustaining $60
- ☐ Contributing $100
- ☐ Benefactor .... $250+
- ☐ Corporate .... $500/$1,000
- ☐ Life $1,000

Enclosed are dues of $_____ and a Special Contribution of $_____

Name _____

Address _____

_____ Zip Code _____

Make checks payable to the CONNECTICUT FOREST AND PARK ASSOCIATION, INC., 16 Meriden Rd., Middletown, CT 06457.

Dues in excess of $6.00 per year, and contributions are deductible from your Federal Taxable Income. Bequests are deductible for Federal Estate Tax purposes.

TRAILS

"A Good Trailsman Always Leaves a Trail a Little Better Than He Finds It."

— EDGAR L. HEERMANCE
(1876–1953)

(Former Secretary, Connecticut Forest
And Park Association, and "Father"
of the Connecticut Blue Trail System)

AMERICAN LEGION AND PEOPLES FOREST TRAILS

(U.S.G.S. quadrangles: Winsted, New Hartford)

The two State Forests lie in the town of Barkhamsted on opposite sides of the West Branch of the Farmington River. The approach to both of them is through the village of Pleasant Valley, which is on Rt. 181 1 m. N of Rt. 44. The American Legion Forest is approached by going N on West River Rd. To reach the Peoples Forest, cross the River on Rt. 181 and immediately turn L on East River Rd. Greenwoods Rd., the main road through the Peoples Forest starts on the right 1 m. N of Rt. 181. Both West and East River Roads terminate in Riverton, 5 m. N of Pleasant Valley. This makes possible a round-trip drive through the two forests.

The American Legion Forest was acquired in 1927 through a gift from the Connecticut Department of the American Legion. The Peoples Forest was acquired in 1923 by public subscription through the efforts of the Connecticut Forest and Park Association.

The Peoples Forest has a network of interesting trails, marked with distinctive colors, named for persons who took an active part in developing the Forest. The American Legion Forest has one trail. See map American Legion and Peoples State Forests. On that map the trails are designated by different symbols, identified in the legend.

HENRY BUCK TRAIL

The Henry Buck Trail was named for Henry R. Buck, engineer of the C.C.C. and vice-president of the Connecticut Forest and Park Association. Start from site of foot bridge on West River Rd. (2.5 m. from Pleasant Valley). The trail leads up through a beautiful forest with outstanding spring wildflowers to the ruins of a cheesebox mill at .77 m., reaches stone terrace with Buck Memorial Tablet at .97 m., an outlook at 1.07 m., passes over ledges to spring pipe at 1.85 m., and reaches River Rd. at 1.99 m.

AGNES BOWEN TRAIL

The trail (orange markers) starts at former Nature Museum and crosses Greenwoods Rd. at .13 m., crosses a brook twice and reaches Stocking Picnic Area at .56 m. It passes several charcoal hearths and crosses the Charles Pack Trail at 1.23 m. At 1.9 m. it crosses Beaver Brook Rd. and at 2.1 m. crosses Greenwoods Rd. At 2.17 m. it crosses the Ross Trail and reaches East River Rd. at 2.69 m.

ELLIOTT BRONSON TRAIL

The trail (red markers) leaves Greenwoods Rd. at parking area near former Nature Museum and goes through the S portion of the forest, crossing a 60 ft. cliff with a good view at .86 m. At 1.63 m. it passes an Indian cave area and reaches Park Rd. near Rt. 181 at 2.02 m.

CHARLES PACK TRAIL

The trail (yellow markers) starts at Greenwoods Rd. near King Rd., crosses the Agnes Bowen Trail at .11 m. and Beaver Brook at .19 m. It crosses Pack Grove Rd. at .82 m. and again at 1.3 m., reaching Beaver Brook Rd. (picnicking) at 1.51 m., Big Spring at 2.07 m. and Greenwoods Rd. at 2.09 m.

JESSIE GIRARD TRAIL

The trail (yellow markers) starts from the old Indian settlement known as Barkhamsted Lighthouse. The nucleus of this settlement was the high-spirited Molly Barber of Wethersfield, who, when crossed by her father in a love affair, eloped with the Indian, Chaugham. Stage drivers, pointing to the light from Chaugham cabin, would shout to their passengers, "There's Barkhamsted Lighthouse; only five more miles to New Hartford."

The trail climbs to the Overlook at 1.11 m. with a grand view. Standing on a bare granite ledge, one looks SE over the Farmington River Valley to a line of hills twenty miles distant. In winter, water falling over the R wall at the Stone Stairs freezes into a solid mass of blue-green ice with formations and colorings like those found in the Alps. At 1.41 m. is an eminence known as

Chaugham Lookout with a remarkable view to the NW. The valley of the West Branch is spread out for 15 m. N from Riverton. The trail keeps on between the Veeder Boulders at 1.56 m. to Greenwoods Rd. at 1.88 m.

ROBERT ROSS TRAIL

The trail (blue markers) begins at the former Nature Museum, reaches a side trail to picnic area at .43 m., passes charcoal hearths, and comes to King Rd. turnaround at .88 m. At 1.39 m. it crosses the Agnes Bowen Trail, a brook at 1.44 m., and reaches the Jessie Girard Trail at 1.75 m., which it follows to 2.12 m. and turns R to Warner Rd. at 2.19 m.

APPALACHIAN TRAIL

(U.S.G.S. quadrangles: Dover Plains, N.Y., Kent, Ellsworth, Cornwall, South Canaan, Sharon, Bashbish Falls, MA. The route of the trail on the U.S.G.S. maps is out of date.)

The Appalachian Trail in Connecticut is part of the through route from Springer Mountain, in Georgia, to Mt. Katahdin, in Maine, a total distance of approximately 2100 miles. The Connecticut section extends for 51 miles from the New York state line at Sherman to the Massachusetts state line at Salisbury *It is marked by white paint blazes.*

The trail goes up the Housatonic River Valley and twice crosses the river. The region is noted for varying forested hills, open valleys, ravines, viewpoints and rugged rocky hills. Interesting features include hardwood and conifer stands, also a large variety of wildflowers and other plants.

The area was formerly the scene of industry. Water power was utilized to operate iron furnaces and the forested hills provided charcoal to feed them. Along the trail may be seen many flat circular areas (hearths where the cut logs were stacked for burning into charcoal). Industry has left the valley; the forested hills remain.

There are shelters at various points along the route.

For detailed description and other information

concerning the Appalachian Trail see *Guide to the Appalachian Trail in Massachusetts-Connecticut* obtainable from the Appalachian Trail Conference, Inc., Box 807, Harpers Ferry, W. Va. 25425.

The description of the route through Connecticut is divided into four sections. The one from Rt. 4 to the "Iron Bridge" is a relocation, opened in May 1988. The former route between these two points, on the east side of the Housatonic R., was converted to the blue-blazed Mohawk Trail, described in a later chapter.

N.Y. LINE TO RT. 341, KENT

- 0.0 Trail enters Conn. at Hoyt Rd., which begins at Rt. 55, ¼ m. W of state line.
- 0.7 Cross Rt. 55. *No parking here.*
- 1.8 Top of Ten Mile Hill.
- 2.9 Ned Anderson Bridge across Ten Mile River. (Camping in field S of bridge.)
- 3.9 Bulls Bridge Rd. *(Parking)* [Watch for future relocation.]
- 5.1 Trail turns R at Dogtail Corners.
- 6.5 Trail leaves rd. and enters woods.
- 7.8 NY/CT line painted on rock. (Not true boundary.)
- 7.9 Indian Rocks—views. [Part of Schaghticoke Indian Reservation.]
- 8.4 Rattlesnake Den campsite.
- 10.1 Thayer Brook.
- 11.0 Side trail to Mt. Algo Lean-to (camping).
- 11.3 Rt. 341 (Kent is 0.8 m. E (R).)

RT. 341 TO RT. 4

- 0.0 Cross Rt. 341 into pasture.
- 0.1 Cross Macedonia Brook on bridge.
- 0.6 Side trail to Numeral Rock.
- 2.8 Cross Skiff Mtn. Rd.
- 3.5 Caleb's Peak (1,160 ft.)—fine views.
- 4.2 St. John's Ledges—fine views.
- 4.6 River Rd. *(Ample parking)* Trail turns L and follows rd.
- 5.6 Trail passes through gate at site of North Kent Bridge, which was washed out in 1930's. Original trail crossed river here.
- 6.9 Stewart Hollow Brook Lean-to (camping).
- 7.3 Stony Brook camping area.

9.6	Trail leaves rd. just before good spring.
10.6	Side trail to Silver Hill Shelter.
11.5	Rt. 4. *(Ample parking downhill to R at jct. with Rt. 7.)*

RT. 4 TO IRON BRIDGE AT FALLS VILLAGE

0.0	Cross Rt. 4 diagonally to L.
0.1	Cross Guinea Brook. (During high water this crossing can be avoided by following Rt. 4 to R to a dirt road on L, which rejoins trail on other side of brook.)
0.2	Cross dirt Old Sharon Rd. (Blue-blazed Mohawk Trail begins here and leads E 1 m. to Cornwall Bridge—*see separate description.*)
1.4	Hatch Brook.
1.5	Pine Knob Loop Trail enters from R.—*see separate description.* It co-exists with the A.T. for 0.8 m.
2.3	Pine Knob Loop Trail leaves A.T. with R. turn.
5.1	Cross Sharon-West Cornwall Rd.
6.1	Pine Swamp Brook Shelter (camping).
7.1	Cross State Forest rd.
7.5	Mt. Easter
8.7	Side trail to Sharon Mtn. campsite.
11.6	Side trail to Belter campsite.
12.3	Rt. 7. Trail skirts edge of cornfield.
12.4	Cross Housatonic River on highway bridge (Rt. 7).
12.6	Junction with Mohawk Trail on Warren Tpk. just N of High School in Falls Village.
13.4	Trail enters woods on L. [It follows route designated "River Trail" in previous editions of *Walk Book.*]
14.7	"Iron Bridge" across Housatonic River.

IRON BRIDGE TO SAGE'S RAVINE

0.0	Trail crosses "Iron Bridge" and immediately turns R and follows river N. Trail comes out to rd. briefly and reenters woods towards dam. [Watch for future relocation.]
0.3	Sugar Hill Rd.
1.2	Turnaround at end of Sugar Hill Rd. *(Parking)*
1.9	Side trail to Limestone Spring Lean-to (camping).
2.5	Side trails to Prospect Mtn. (R) and Rand's

View (straight). A.T. turns L. [If coming from N, watch for future relocation here.]
- 3.4 "Billy's View"
- 5.2 Summit of Barrack Matiff (derivation unknown).
- 5.8 Trail turns L on Rt. 44 for short distance to next R turn. [Watch for future relocation.]
- 6.4 Trail turns R on Rt. 41.
- 6.6 Trailhead at *parking area.*
- 6.8 Plateau campsite.
- 8.7 Jct. with Lion's Head Trail.
- 8.9 Summit of Lion's Head (1,738 ft.)—good views.
- 9.4 Side trail to Bald Peak (1 m.)
- 9.6 Riga campsite.
- 10.3 Ball Brook campsite.
- 10.9 Bond Shelter (camping) at Brassie Brook.
- 11.3 Riga Junction: Undermountain Trail leads R 1.9 m. to Rt. 41.
- 11.5 Bear Mtn. Rd.
- 12.2 Summit of Bear Mtn. (2,316 ft.)—excellent views.
- 13.0 Sage's Ravine campsites. (Caretaker on duty in summer and on fall week-ends.)
- 13.4 Trail crosses Sage's Ravine Brook into Massachusetts.

CHATFIELD TRAIL

(U.S.G.S. quadrangle: Clinton)

The trail begins on Rt. 80 (1.35 m. W of Rt. 81 in Killingworth, 2.55 m. E of Rt. 79). Trail enters wood road S of Rt. 80 .1 m. W of Chatfield Hollow State Park exit road. At .05 m. it leaves wood road, passes over ledges and arrives at nose of large ledge at .32 m. Trail passes a spring (sometimes dry) at .47 m. and then through large hemlock and under a ledge at .73 m., where large ice falls form in winter.

Trail turns R through a pine forest, passes a bog, and then arrives at ledge with glacial boulders at 1.14 m. (views to the S). At 1.28 m. trail arrives at ledge overhang with caves. (Short side trail passes through cave.) At 1.43 m. trail turns L onto old road and intersects with an alternate trail at 1.44 m. (Alternate proceeds R, around a swamp, and by a small fall. It then proceeds downhill following state forest boundary markers, across a brook, and ascends to bottom of cliff.

Trail then descends to Champlin Rd. [dirt] which it follows to main trail. This trail makes a nice loop for day hikers from Chatfield Hollow State Park, about .5 m. in length).

Main trail then proceeds on old road, turns L at 1.45 m. and arrives at Feather Ledge at 1.71 m. Trail turns L along top of ledge, then descends steeply, swings R around base of ledge, and arrives back on old road at 2 m. It turns L, enters Champlin Rd. (where the alternate comes back) and follows it L, turns R at 2.13 m., crosses brook at 2.23 m. and enters Deer Lake Camp at 2.29 m., turns R off old road and arrives at large rock overhang at 2.79 m. It leaves ledges, turns R, then L on old road, turns sharp R at 3.37 m. (*Do not follow on old road; please stay on blue-blazed trail.*) Trail crosses small brook at 3.52 m. and crosses second brook before coming to a dirt rd. at 3.9 m. It turns R across bridge and R again into woods. From there it follows E bank of Chatfield Hollow Br. to River Rd. at 4.33 m. (1.4 m. SE to Green Hill Rd. in Killingworth).

Chatfield Hollow Trails

The Department of Environmental Protection has an expanded system of trails at Chatfield Hollow State Park. This system does not lend itself to inclusion in this publication.

COCKAPONSET FOREST TRAILS

(U.S.G.S. quadrangles: Clinton, Haddam)

Both the Killingworth Block (which includes Chatfield Hollow State Park) and the Turkey Hill Block of the Cockaponset State Forest contain trails. Some of these trails were constructed in 1934–35 by the C.C.C. and the stone steps and stone culverts can still be seen.

COCKAPONSET TRAIL

(U.S.G.S. quadrangle: Haddam)

The Cockaponset Trail starts at the junction of Rt. 148 and Filley Rd. (paved forest rd.) in Chester (2.6 m. E of Rt. 81 and 2.6 m. W of exit 6 from Rt. 9). This main trail provides a route N passing the Pataconk Reservoir (parking, picnic tables, fireplaces, and swimming areas) Old County

Rd., Jericho Rd. and ends on Beaver Meadow Rd. (Haddam paved rd.) a quarter mile W of exit 8 on Rt. 9. See map Cockaponset Forest Trails.

COCKAPONSET TRAIL
(blue paint blazes)

Point No.		Miles
1.	Route 148 — State Highway in Chester	.00
2.	South Pataconk Junction — *Pataconk trail	.10
3.	Crosses Filley Rd. (parking & picnic areas)	1.69
4.	Pataconk Crossover — *Pataconk trail	1.80
5.	Pataconk Brook — *Pataconk trail	2.85
6.	North Pataconk Junction — *Pataconk trail	3.18
7.	Old County Rd. — (gravel forest rd.)	3.96
8.	Old County Rd. Junction — *Old Forest trail	4.10
9.	Jericho Junction — *Old Forest trail	4.75
10.	Jericho Rd. (gravel — west crossing)	5.00
11.	Wildwood Junction — *Wildwood trail	5.05
12.	Jericho Rd. — (gravel — middle crossing)	6.03
13.	Jericho Rd — (gravel — east crossing)	6.81
14.	Beaver Brook Junction — *Wildwood trail	7.33
15.	Beaver Meadow Rd. — Haddam paved rd.	7.53

Alternate trails beginning and ending on the Cockaponset trail make circuit walks of varying lengths possible with a minimum retracing of steps. Connecting points marked (*) above.

ALTERNATE TRAILS

(red dots on blue paint blazes)

Pataconk Trail — Point 2 to Point 4 is 1.64 m.; Point 4 to Point 5 is 1.03 m.; Point 5 to Point 6 is .19 m.

Old Forest Trail — Point 8 to Point 9 is .48 m.

Wildwood Trail — Point 11 to Point 14 is 1.4 m.

FALLS BROOK TRAIL

(U.S.G.S. quadrangle: West Granville, MA)

The western block of Tunxis Forest is worth exploring. From West Hartland drive N 2.5 m.

on Rt. 20 where a Blue Trail leads S through the woods to Falls Brook. Entrance is on the S side of Rt. 20 about .5 m. uphill (W) of the lookout over the reservoir. Follow brook S .5 m. to two small but beautiful falls, the lower one about 50 ft. high. See map Tunxis Trail, N of Route 44.

GAY CITY TRAILS
GAY CITY TO GLASTONBURY FIRE TOWER
(U.S.G.S. quadrangle: Marlborough)

The colony known as Gay City was started by Elijah Andrus in 1796. In about 1800 John Gay was officially appointed president of the colony and soon the Gays were in the majority of the twenty-five families who settled there.

A few families left in 1804 to settle nearer the Connecticut River, not taking kindly to the compulsory church service twice a week. But the remaining families settled down and built a thriving town. There was a saw mill, a couple of grist mills and a large woolen mill, later used for the manufacturing of satinette. This mill beside the Blackledge River burned to the ground in the summer of 1830 and its ruins are a landmark on the blue trail. The settlement continued until the time of the Civil War.

The old cemetery, pond, ruins of the woolen mill, overgrown canal that brought water from the pond to the mill's overshot wheel, and cellars of former Gay City houses are all that remain of this once thriving community. This area is now the Gay City State Park with facilities for picnicking and bathing. The entrance to the park is on Rt. 85 about .75 m. S of the Bolton-Hebron town line.

The original trails in the Gay City area are blue-blazed. A network of numbered trails has been added to the blue trails by the Department of Environmental Protection. These new trails, together with the blue trails, make possible many interesting walks of varying difficulty. The blue trails are described in detail below and the new numbered trails are described briefly. See map Shenipsit Trail #2.

NORTH TRAIL

This blue-blazed trail follows the old Gay City Rd., once the main route from Glastonbury to

Gay City. Leaving Rt. 85 at the park entrance, the trail follows the paved road to the toll house. At .14 m. is an old graveyard with several stones dating back to the early 19th century. At .16 m. trail #8 branches R. The blue trail divides at .31 m., the Pond Loop going R.

(Data for the Pond Loop are: Starting from the North Trail, the trail follows an old dirt road and reaches clearing at the parking lot at .19 m., continues through the main picnic area and reaches pond at the beach. To the R (N) Trails #7 and #9 leave the N end of the pond. The Pond Loop turns L at the swimming area, heads S along the shore to the dam where Trail #6 crosses the bridge over the dam. Here the Pond Loop turns L and follows the old aqueduct to the ruins of the mill, crosses the tailrace from the mill at .57 m. and rejoins the North Trail at .61 m.)

Going straight ahead from the first Pond Loop Junction the North Trail descends to the second Pond Loop Junction at .51 m. and crosses the Blackledge River at .52 m. Just across the river at .54 m. is the eastern South Trail Junction.

The North Trail climbs gradually, bears R from the tote road to an earth dam at .66 m. Crossing the dam, the trail reenters the woods at .71 m. and climbs, reaching an old cellar hole on L at .82 m. Descending slightly, Trail #5 enters R at .86 m. Still descending, a small brook is crossed at .91 m., shortly after which the trail starts to climb, leveling off at 1.15 m., and crosses a brook just before reaching the western South Trail Junction at 1.20 m.

From Junction the North Trail continues W, crossing a gas pipe line at 1.39 m. Then it climbs more steeply. At 1.7 m. it turns sharp R. The North Trail ends at Birch Mtn. Rd. (2.1 m.) at a point about 0.5 m. N of the Glastonbury fire tower.

SOUTH TRAIL

The South Trail is a U-shaped route that connects with the North Trail at two points. The eastern South Trail Junction is on the W side of the Blackledge River.

The South Trail skirts an overgrown clearing (old cellar hole on R) and follows an old tote rd. S. After a moderate ascent the trail descends to a brook crossing at .43 m. (Beaver activity is evident to the R along this brook.) The trail climbs gradually to the junction with the Brimstone Trail. (This is Trail #10, which goes back to the North Trail at the first Pond Loop Junction, 1.5 m.)

From the junction the South Trail bears R and goes SW until it turns sharply N at .83 m. and reaches a trail junction at .86 m. [Formerly the South Trail continued W from this junction 1.3 m. to the Glastonbury fire tower but is now abandoned.] From this former trail junction the South Trail continues N to a height of land at 1.05 m. and then descends, crossing a brook and a swampy area at 1.4 m. It reaches the western South Trail Junction with the North Trail at 1.7 m. (This Junction is 0.66 m. from the Eastern Junction, via the North Trail.)

NUMBERED TRAILS

Trail #1 — (Daily Rd.) Trail leaves the L side of Rt. 85 .5 m. N of the park entrance. Trail follows the old Daily Rd. W on level terrain. Swinging to the NW Trail #8 enters on the L at .44 m. The Blackledge River is crossed on old bridge at .68 m. (old dam site R) and Trail #7 enters L at .71 m. At .83 m. trail leaves state land, going uphill with farm fields on each side of trail and ends on French Rd. at 1.01 m.

Trail #2 — (North Trail) Blue-blazed. See above.

Trail #3 — (South Trail) Blue-blazed. See above.

Trail #4 — (Crossover Trail) This trail is now part of the South Trail.

Trail #5 — (French Rd.) Trail bears R from North Trail and follows old road N along ridge. Trail #6 enters from R at .36 m. Trail crosses brook and continues N to paved portion of French Rd. at .76 m.

Trail #6 — (Bridge) Trail leaves the Pond loop at the dam. After crossing the bridge, trail enters woods and climbs ridge. Trail turns N and descends at .8 m., then turns W at .13 m. and ascends past cascades and joins Trail #5 at .28 m.

Trail #7 — (Possum) Trail leaves lower parking lot N of swimming area. Crossing brook and entering woods trail bears L (Trail #9 R). At .16 m. trail crosses bridge over Blackledge

River and climbs rise. Descending to the N at .41 m., trail continues to intersection of Trail #1 at .61 m.

Trail #8 — (Bolton) Trail leaves park road just beyond the Gay City graveyard. Entering the woods at an open field, the trail heads N through the woods. Trail #9 enters L at .67 m. Trail crosses stream and continues N to Trail #1 at .75 m.

Trail #9 — (Partridge) Trail leaves lower parking lot at same location as Trail #7. Trail bears R, climbs gradually through the woods, turning N at .36 m. and intersecting Trail #8 at .44 m.

Trail #10 — (Brimstone) Trail leaves the North Trail on the L just beyond the first Pond Loop Junction. At first it follows an old tote rd. The Trail continues generally S, and reaches the Blackledge River at 1.2 m. It crosses river and climbs NW crossing a brook below a small falls and reaches the South Trail at 1.5 m.

HOUSATONIC RANGE TRAIL

(U.S.G.S. quadrangles: New Milford, Kent)

The Housatonic Range Trail follows the general route of an old Indian trail above the Housatonic River, parallel to U.S. 7. A good day hike including some occasionally steep climbing and a few areas of rough "scramblin" through areas of ledges and boulders, the trail is crossed by Rt. 37 and Squash Hollow Rd. in two locations (parking). The trail passes through wooded areas with a good mixture of hardwoods and evergreens.

As a result of extensive quarry excavations since 1987, the southern section of the trail no longer connects with U.S. Rt. 7. Instead the section of trail over Pine Knob and Candlewood Mtn. has been made into a loop by marking a new trail east of the ridge.

Parking for several cars is available at the Rt. 37 trailhead, just E of the jct. of Rt. 37 and Candlewood Mtn. Rd. Parking is also available adjacent to the old Gaylordsville cemetery near the N end of the trail. See map Housatonic Range Trail.

The loop trail starts at the Rt. 37 parking area. It enters woods next to a large boulder and heads S. It passes through mixed forest of hardwoods and evergreens for .25 m. and then winds out on top of rock ledge overlook (clearing) with small stand of cathedral white pines. Trail goes down off ledge into clearing, where it splits, the E branch being the new trail along the E side of the ridge: *look for loop sign.*

The E branch goes down along seasonal runoff for about 75 yd., before turning S to run parallel to slope of ridge. A switchback at .5 m. gives access to gradual ascent. At .8 m the trail leads across open rock ledge with good views of Rt. 7 and Housatonic R. valley.

The trail continues S with some gradual changes in elevation, until at about 1.4 m. it leads down slope through boulder field and on to shoulder of Candlewood Mtn. It continues through a mostly level area of hardwood. At 1.7 m. a spur trail leads directly to Kelly's Slide—easier access from summit of Candlewood Mtn. (see below). Trail continues to base of mountain and through boulder fall at bottom of Kelly's Slide (several interesting boulder caves). It then starts slow ascent of east slope of Candlewood Mtn. The trail winds through a heavy stand of mountain laurel, crosses an open rock ledge, and then gradually ascends to summit of Candlewood Mtn. (991 ft.) at 2.2 m.

Trail descends from summit, then reaches junction with short loop trail at 2.45 m. (Loop leads to Kelly's Slide—good views.). Main trail continues (loop trail rejoins at 2.55 m.) and crosses "Paradise Valley" a saddle between Candlewood Mtn. and Pine Knob. Trail reaches summit of Pine Knob at 2.75 m. Trail descends "corkscrew," steep ledges and tumbled boulders, continues through hemlocks, and crosses brook at 3.27 m. It passes overhanging rock and cave, and descends to Rt. 37 at 3.65 m.

From Rt. 37 trail turns L (W) and follows along highway several hundred ft. and turns R into woods. Trail crosses stream at 3.88 m. and climbs through tumbled boulders to Suicide Ledges at 4.2 m., descends steeply, passes enormous stone wall and reaches Squash Hollow Rd. at 4.77 m.

Trail follows road to L (N) for 50 ft. then turns R into woods and through seasonal wetland before joining wood road at 4.88 m.

The Tories Cave Trail turns R at 5.35 m. (This is a short trail leading to a cave of several small rooms. Lights needed.) From the cave it continues about 300 ft. E to U.S. 7. A branch of the trail rejoins the main trail at 5.58 m.

Trail crosses Squash Hollow Rd. again at 6.21 m., turns L on Squash Hollow Rd. about 500 ft. and then R (N) into woods. Trail climbs to The Pinnacle (Strait's Rock), a large flat rock and cliff at 7.28 m., and descends steeply through hemlocks, around and down over large boulders. The trail gradually winds W, eventually crossing brook and ending across from the Gaylordsville Cemetery at about 8 m.

KETTLETOWN STATE PARK

(U.S.G.S. quadrangle: Southbury)

Access to the three trails in Kettletown State Park is from the Park entrance on George's Hill Rd., Southbury. *(Parking fee from Memorial Day to Labor Day.)* There is also access to the S end of the Pomperaug Trail from Jackson Cove Recreation Area, at the S end of Jackson Cove Rd., Oxford. *(Parking fee or permit from Memorial Day to Labor Day.)* See map Kettletown State Park.

POMPERAUG TRAIL

(Blazes: blue; Description: N to S)

Follow park road from ticket booth at entrance, taking first left fork and continuing to bridge over Kettletown Brook at 0.25 m. Just past the bridge turn L from the rd. and follow trail with quick R and L turns on old rds. Turn L at 0.35 m. to enter woods, then turn R, using a stone wall to bridge a wet area. Next ascend gradually to jct. with N end of Crest Trail at 0.85 m. *(See description following.)*

Continue southerly through laurel groves at 1.25 and 1.35 m. At 1.65 m. pass viewpoint to E, followed by a gradual descent through a laurel grove at 1.70 m. Pass S end of Crest Trail at 1.95 m. Start a steep descent to shore of Lake Zoar at

2.20 m. and reach end of trail at Jackson Cove Rd. at 2.55 m.

The trail is located within the Park, except for the S end at the Jackson Cove Recreation Area. A loop trip is possible by returning via the Crest Trail, which adds 0.10 m. to the round trip distance.

CREST TRAIL

(Blazes: blue/white dot; Description: N to S)

Trail branches from SW side of Pomperaug Trail at a point 0.85 m. from its beginning. *(See above.)* At 0.20 m. turn L. *(Connector back to campground—blue blazes—continues straight.)* Cross over stone wall at 0.30 m. and come to viewpoint over Lake Zoar at 0.70 m. Go through laurel grove at 0.90 m. After descending on rocks and through a grove, turn L and ascend to jct. with the Pomperaug Trail at 1.20 m. *(See above.)*

MILLER TRAIL

(Blazes: blue; Description: clockwise)

This trail, located in the NW section of the Park, is a full loop following an old road. It is a good cross-country ski trail. A side trail leads to a scenic overlook of Lake Zoar.

The trail starts at a gate opposite the beginning of a loop on the picnic area road, 0.45 m. SW of the ticket booth at the Park entrance. Make a short ascent to the main loop trail (0.50 m.) and turn L. After a R turn make a steep ascent to jct. with a side trail *(blazes: blue/white dots)* on L at 0.80 m., which leads 0.20 m. to overlook of Lake Zoar to the SW. From the overlook go back to the main loop trail, turn L and return to the campground road at 1.55 m.

LILLINONAH TRAIL

(U.S.G.S. quadrangle: Newtown)

Trail is in the Upper Paugussett State Forest. Access: In Newtown take The Boulevard N off Rt. 6 between I-84 and Rt. 25. In 1.5 m. Hanover Rd. enters from L and continues straight ahead.

LILLINONAH TRAIL 17

At 5.0 m. come to Pond Brook and a State Boat Launch area. The Lillinonah Trail makes a circuit in a clockwise direction: N along Pond Brook to Lake Lillinonah, then E and S along the Lake to Alberts Hill Rd, from which it returns W along the Forest boundary to the starting point. *The trail is closed in winter — from mid-December to mid-March.* (A forest rd. traverses the forest from Alberts Hill Rd. to Hanover Rd.) See map Lillinonah Trail.

0.0	From Hanover Rd. 0.1 m. S of Pond Brook crossing, follow trail parallel to brook through mixed forest.
0.5	Continue along a wide inlet, climbing slightly.
0.9	Reach hemlock knoll as Pond Brook enters Lake Lillinonah. (In the middle of the Lake near this point is the corner of Fairfield, New Haven and Litchfield counties.) Descend and continue along lake shore.
1.6	Go R and begin ascent.
1.8	Reach a large oak, 250 ft. above the lake, and continue at same level.
2.3	Descend steeply to lake shore.
2.5	Turn inland and climb.
2.6	Reach elevation 120 ft. above lake.
3.0	Turn L. (100 ft ahead on R is a "clear-cut" area, with a descriptive sign. This area has been planted with black walnut trees.)
3.1	Pass picnic spot overlooking lake. Climb slightly and then descend.
3.5	Reach shore.
3.6	Turn L on old rd. to picnic spots on shore. Continue along shore.
4.0	Trail ends at Alberts Hill Rd. To return to starting point, turn R on Alberts Hill Rd.
4.2	Pass sugarbush enhancement area on R.
4.3	Take L fork past small green with village pump and turn R on Sanford Rd.
4.4	Turn R thru wooden gate onto forest rd. and then turn L on new trail.
4.8	Jog to R to cross small stream; return and continue to L (west) thru hardwood forest.
4.9	Turn R (north) uphill thru hemlocks.
5.0	Turn L (west) along side of hill; then turn L and down across a draw.
5.1	Reach top of small ridge and go R (north) thru a draw.

5.2 Make sharp R turn up to ridge top and then turn L thru hemlocks.
5.3 Descend into hardwood area heavily logged in 1988.
5.6 Pass two old deer stands; then climb small rocky pinnacle and descend along stone wall.
5.7 Turn L on unpaved forest rd.
5.9 Turn R on paved Hanover Rd.
6.1 Reach starting point of trail.

MACEDONIA BROOK STATE PARK TRAILS

(U.S.G.S. quadrangles: Ellsworth, Amenia, N.Y.)

There are 13 m. of marked foot trails in the park, including the CCC rd. In addition, the gravel auto rd. provides good walking. All trails cross or meet the Macedonia Ridge Trail, whose oval loop encompasses much of the 2300-acre park. In general, the trails to the E of the park rd. are less steep than those to the W. With the exception of the Green Trail, all trails originate on the park rd. (Macedonia Brook Rd.)

Stop at the camping office beside the rd. at the southern end of the park for trail map with history of this interesting area, camping permits and information. See map Macedonia Ridge Trail.

Most descriptions start from access points on automobile rd.:

Green Trail on E side of park (note that Pine Hill Trail on W is also green-blazed; these two do not connect directly) begins from Orange Trail (see below), follows overgrown woods rd. up to Macedonia Ridge Trail at 0.5 m., then on to Fuller Mt. Rd. at 1.0 m. where log barrier closes woods rd. to cars.

Orange Trail bears E from park rd. 0.3 m. N of camp office, halfway between last "no camping" picnic area on W and park sign on E saying "Campground Begins" (an unmarked feeder trail near the latter sign leads to Orange Trail in about 100 yds.). Orange Trail passes a spring, follows a woods rd. Green Trail goes off R through break in old stone wall at 0.2 m. Orange Trail continues on level, just above park's easternmost campsites (feeder trails to some of these); at 0.5 m. reaches old bridge site and nearly returns to park rd., then bears R and ascends steeply; levels off, passing several old charcoal mounds. Meets Macedonia Ridge Trail (an abandoned rd.) at 1.2 m. Turns L and follows old rd. to "4 corners" (campground cluster) at 1.3 m. Follows old Chipewalla Rd. (passable by car) to jct. of Macedonia Ridge Trail and old CCC rd. at 1.6 m.

CCC Road (once called Sharon Rd.). Closed to vehicles, the northern end of this grassy rd. bears W from the northern park boundary sign on Weber Rd. where Macedonia Ridge Trail crosses rd., and runs roughly parallel to park rd. but at slightly higher elevation, past park offices at 1.7 m., returning to park rd. at 1.8 m. The dry-laid stonework, built by CCC workers in 1933–35 with evident pride and skill, and the lush varieties of ferns are special joys of this gentle walk. Macedonia Ridge Trail (blue) crosses at 0.3 m.; Pine Hill (green) Trail at 0.9 m.; Cobble Mt. (white) Trail at 1.6 m.

Pine Hill Trail ("Foil Trail" in former *Walk Books*), green-blazed, leaves W side of park rd. at old woods rd. with log barrier 0.8 m. N of camping office (green blaze on tree is difficult to spot from car). Trail jogs L slightly at CCC Rd., bears R into woods, and joins Macedonia Ridge Trail at 0.5 m. Turn R to ascend Pine Hill; turn L to ascend Cobble Mt.

Cobble Mt. Trail, white-blazed, leads W from park rd. at trail sign, 0.1 m. N of camp office. Crosses brook on bridge, joins CCC rd. briefly, then cuts L into woods. White trail climbs steeply to jct. with Macedonia Ridge Trail just below summit of Cobble Mt. R on Macedonia Ridge Trail leads to summit in 0.1 m.; L to park rd. in 1.6 m.

MACEDONIA RIDGE TRAIL

(U.S.G.S. quadrangles: Ellsworth, Amenia, N.Y.)

The Macedonia Ridge Trail includes sections of the former Appalachian Trail in Macedonia

Brook State Park plus sections of other park trails. It is a loop trail beginning and ending near the southern end of the park. A relocation that makes the trail 0.5 m. longer was made in 1990 to avoid the red pine harvest area between Keeler and Weber Roads.

See map Macedonia Ridge Trail. Description that follows is in a counterclockwise direction.

0.0	From Park rd. cross bridge over brook on dirt rd. In 100' trail enters woods on L and slabs side of hill.
0.5	Turn sharp L and climb ridge.
0.9	Jct. of Yellow Trail — leads L to park pavilion.
1.3	Jct. with Green Trail coming from W.
1.4	Fork, bear L. Green Trail goes R.
2.2	Turn L on abandoned rd. (To R it leads to Dolldorf Rd.).
2.3	At rd. barricade Blue Trail turns R and crosses brook. Trail ahead and to L is Orange Trail.
2.7	Turn L on dirt Keeler Rd., cross bridge and turn R.
2.8	Relocated trail follows W bank of Macedonia Br.
2.9	Pass thru stone wall and begin ascent.
3.2	From top of hill (good views) begin steep descent by switchbacks.
3.3	Reach bottom of steep section.
3.4	Turn L on dirt Weber Rd. and then R on to old CCC rd.
3.8	Turn R uphill on old Chippewalla Rd. (old stagecoach rd. from Dover to Kent).
3.9	Rd. levels off. Trail turns L and ascends slope of Pine Hill.
4.1	Reach outlook on Pine Hill (good view).
4.4	At jct. with Pine Hill Trail (formerly known as Foil Trail), cross the col and ascend. (The trail up Cobble Mt. is very steep with many large rocks and should be negotiated with caution, especially in wet weather.)
5.0	Reach crest of Cobble Mt. (1,380', private property. Here are splendid views to the W of the Catskills, across Chickadee Valley, and of the Taconic range to the N. At the bottom of the ledge the Cobble Mt. trail descends steeply to a picnic area of the park.) Descend S slope of Cobble Mt.

5.4	Jct. of unmarked trail to the L — connects with Cobble Mt. trail. Begin ascent of South Cobble Mt.
6.1	Reach outlook on South Cobble.
6.3	At this point trail turns L, crosses brook on bridge and descends to rd.
6.7	Trail ends at parking area next to rd., where it began.

McLEAN GAME REFUGE TRAILS

The McLean Game Refuge is located just off Rt. 10, .5 m. S of Granby and 5 m. N of Simsbury. The Refuge consists of about 4500 acres of rolling woodland, meadows and streams. Within it is one of the Barndoor Hills with good viewpoints. There are two picnic areas and 20 miles of trails. The Refuge is open from 10 A.M. to 6 P.M. The parking area convenient to the trails lies outside the gate. Dogs must be kept on the leash at all times. Smoking and building of fires are prohibited outside the main picnic area except by special permission of caretaker. Mr. George P. McLean wished the Refuge to be "a place where some of the things God made may be seen by those who love them as I love them and who may find in them the peace of mind and body that I have found."

See map McLean Game Refuge.

Note: In addition to the trails described below, three short loop trails (red, yellow, and royal blue), have been marked at the Refuge. A map of these is on display to the L just before the bridge which crosses the outlet to Trout Pond.

EASTERN DIVISION

(U.S.G.S. quadrangle: Tariffville)

The South Trail begins a few feet from the parking lot. It ascends gradually 60 yds. to junction with North Trail. Bear L uphill and continue along plateau with Trout Pond on R. Pass through hemlock and pine forest past S end of Trout Pond, bear L and gradually ascend to Refuge boundary near field at .4 m. Continue on nearly level ground to wood road at .8 m. (Unblazed route, L, leads to Canton Rd.) Continue through

Jack pine to Creek Trail junction at 1.2 m. (Creek Trail, R, descends to and crosses Bissell Brook, reaches the auto drive (Swamp Lane Rd.) at .3 m. and joins the North Trail at the top of the knoll 70 yds. from the drive.) Continue along level on South Trail to junction at 1.7 m. (Wood road L leads to Canton Rd.) Cross wood road and descend to Bissell Brook at 2 m. Trail parallels Bissell Brook and ascends to junction at 2.4 m. (Side trail, straight ahead, leads to Simsbury Rd.) South trail bears R and descends to Bissell Brook at 2.6 m. Cross brook and ascend to Swamp Lane Rd. at 2.7 m. Cross road and descend sharply to level area between two kettles and ascend gradually to junction with North Trail at 3 m. Swamp Lane Rd. is 25 ft. straight ahead.

South Trail Extension begins at a large hemlock tree opposite side trail to South Trail on Simsbury Rd. (County Rd.). It climbs moderately, passing hemlock stand on N side of slope at .1 m., then continues through mature pine and oak stand. Trail descends to pine grove and ascends slightly to oak and hemlock and then to hemlock stand on N slope at .5 m. It continues through hemlock to moderate dip at .8 m., passes through young oak and pine stand and descends to Barndoor Hills Rd. at 1 m. Trail crosses road and ascends steep grade continuing through open oak and pine woodland, then descends to edge of hemlock stand at 1.1 m. It continues through open woodland to area of young pine and hardwood at 1.2 m., ascends slightly through oak to steep rise to ridge at 1.3 m. Trail descends steep hill and continues on level ground through oak and pine stand at 1.4 m. and ascends steep hill and descends sharply to creek at 1.6 m. It crosses creek and continues through pine forest to Firetown Trail at 1.7 m.

The North Trail branches from the South Trail 60 yds. from the latter's beginning. (see above) It parallels the entrance road, crosses it, passes over the bridge over the outlet of Trout Pond and enters wood road R at .2 m. Wood road soon becomes a trail which passes near the West Branch of Salmon Brook and undulates through hardwoods and hemlocks (Cross-over trail to Mt. Rd. provides easy mile walk loop to bridge at pond outlet), across Stony Hill to Mt. Rd. at 1.5 m. Cross and continue on level ground to Summit Trail junction at 1.7 m. (See description below) North Trail bears L, ascends horseback, descends and crosses Mt. Rd. at 2 m., then rises 70 yds. to Creek Trail Junction. (See description under South Trail) North Trail bears R and continues on ridge of horseback. The trail becomes a well-defined wood road and reaches Kettle Pond Trail junction at 2.5 m. (Kettle Pond Trail descends to the pond and rejoins the North Trail at .1 m.) North Trail descends to the southern junction of the Summit Trail at 2.7 m. (Summit Trail to top bear R uphill. Straight ahead it leads to Barndoor Hills Rd.) North Trail bears sharp L into woods, paralleling the wood road just traversed, and descends to Kettle Pond and Kettle Pond Trail junction at 3 m. North Trail bears right, circles W side of the pond and bears R into the woods. Traversing fairly level ground, it reaches the junction of South and Firetown Trails at 4 m. (South Trail bears L. Firetown Trail is straight ahead. R on auto road leads to exit gate and Barndoor Hills Rd. at .2 m.)

The Summit Trail leaves Barndoor Hills Rd. at a barway and reaches the junction of North Trail in 120 yds. (North Trail heading for Kettle Pond Trail and Firetown Trail bears R into woods. North Trail headed for Trout Pond and main entrance gate bears R along wood road.) Summit Trail proceeds straight ahead and ascends wood road sharply to cedar and junction of Peak Loop at .2 m. (Peak Loop bears L and loops around summit, with views to West Granby and other Barndoor Hill and returns to cedar at .4 m.) Summit trail descends, crosses Mt. Rd. at .5 m. and North Trail at .7 m. (North Trail, L, leads to main entrance gate, R, uphill to point near the beginning of Summit Trail and Barndoor Hills Rd.)

WESTERN DIVISION

(U.S.G.S. quadrangles: Tariffville, New Hartford)

The Firetown Trail begins at the western junction of the North and South Trails. In 25 ft. it crosses the auto drive (Barndoor Hills Rd. .2 m. R) and descends to Barndoor Hills Rd. near its junction with Simsbury Rd. Trail descends on road, crosses Simsbury Rd., and enters woods at

.2 m. It ascends a knoll, descends to a pasture and bears R around the latter to ascend another knoll. From here the trail passes over fairly level ground, parallelling the West Branch, to a giant hemlock and wood road at 1.3 m. and junction of East Loop at 1.6 m. (East Loop bears R into woods, traverses fairly level ground and then ascends a ridge which it follows to Firetown Rd. at .7 m. at the boundary between Granby and Simsbury.) Firetown Trail continues on wood road through pastures of old Case Farm to Firetown Rd. at 1.9 m. Trail bears R on Firetown Rd. and reaches a driveway at 2 m. Turn R into driveway and R into woods shortly thereafter. Trail follows well-defined wood road and parallels a brook, reaching West Loop junction at 2.1 m. (West Loop bears R on wood road and climbs fairly steeply to summit with two viewpoints. It then descends steeply, crossing two brooks. At the second brook the trail again becomes a wood road and reaches Broad Hill Trail at 1.8 m. and Firetown Rd. at 2.1 m. (The Broad Hill Trail bears L from West Loop and rises gradually to Broad Hill Rd. at .7 m.) The Firetown Trail continues along brook, passes a wood road entering R, and crosses brook. It continues on wood road to junction of West Ledge Trail at 3.1 m. (West Ledge Trail bears L uphill past old cellar holes to West Ledge Rd. at .7 m.).

MATTABESETT TRAIL

The Mattabesett Trail's three divisions (Eastern, Central, and Northern) are connected by several miles of unblazed paved roads.

The Eastern Division runs between the Connecticut River and Rt. 154 (formerly Rt. 9A). The proposed section from the River to Reservoir Rd. has not yet been built. The completed portion of this Division includes about 7 m. of trail and 5.5 m. of loops. The main Mattabesett Trail is blazed with blue rectangles and the loops with blue circles. In general, the loop trails are on easier grades, and pass fewer points of interest than the main trail. By using both main and loop trails, circuit walks of varying lengths may be taken.

The Central Division is between Rt. 154 and I-91, with about 35 m. of trail and no loops.

The Northern Division is between I-91 and the Wilbur Cross Hwy. (Rt. 15) with about 5 m. of trail and no loops.

From high ledges and bald knobs the Eastern Division provides vistas of the Connecticut River and a picturesque terrain of tumbled ledges, frequent brooks, and shallow bogs. The Central and Northern Divisions offer some of the finest ridge walking and cliff views in the state. Mattabesett was the Indian name for Middletown. See maps Mattabesett Trail, #1 and #2.

Eastern Division
SEVEN FALLS

(U.S.G.S. quadrangle: Middle Haddam)

Park at Seven Falls Roadside Park (unmarked) on Rt. 154 .8 m. S of Aircraft Rd. (end of ramp off Exit 10 on Rt. 9). Trail starts at N end of bridge over Bible Rock Br. and follows it downstream. At .21 m. trail turns sharply up a side stream and crosses brook; it follows upgrade at .43 m. on woods road. Trail ascends on to rock ridge near boundary marker for Middletown/Haddam town line at .61 m., continues through laurel and pitchpine grove. The trail proceeds past a few limited views and interesting overlooks, and at .79 m. crosses power lines with panoramic view (el. 340 ft.). After crossing a second power line, trail descends, winding around boulders, and then ascends to outlook and on up to another outcrop. Following along slope, trail reaches *Hollow Junction* at 1.36 m. (From here the Seven Falls Loop Trail (blue discs) runs W back to Roadside Park.) Trail crosses Freeman Rd. at 1.52 m. and continues to Aircraft Rd. at 1.65 m.

SEVEN FALLS LOOP

The trail descends quickly from *Hollow Junction* along switchbacks, passes through a large stretch of ferns and to the left of a swampy area. After crossing a brook, it climbs to an outcrop overlooking the power line. There the trail turns back, crosses the brook again, and follows the opposite side of the swamp. *(Note: this part floods during spring thaw.)* Trail then turns to power line at 1.02 m., with nice overlook, and meets the main trail just east of Roadside Park.

BEAR HILL

(U.S.G.S. quadrangle: Middle Haddam)

From Aircraft Rd. trail climbs around outcrop to *South Junction* at .11 m. Then it ascends through laurel to a natural footstool on ledge at .26 m. Trail descends past small falls and then follows brook uphill, crossing several times, before leaving it at .78 m. Trail follows base of long ridge, then climbs to an elevation of 450 ft. with a view of the Connecticut River S from Higganum to Salmon River Cove. After following atop Chinese Wall, trail crosses brook at 1.4 m. and climbs over ledges to *South Crossover* at 1.72 m. After descending hill, trail reaches *Summit Junction* at 1.87 m. and *Midway Junction* at 1.98 m. The trail ascends hill, descends and skirts swamp at 2.12 m. Then it turns and ascends to the summit of Bear Hill (el. 660 ft.) at 2.44 m. From the summit the trail passes *North Crossover* at 2.64 m., tops the crest, and descends through a laurel grove. Then it ascends to an overlook above Hubbard Pond at 3.31 m., crosses a brook, and reaches power lines at 3.84 m. Trail passes *North Junction* at second power line at 3.89 m., crosses Bear Hill Rd. at 4.1 m. and descends to Brooks Rd. at 4.31 m.

BEAR HILL LOOP

From *North Junction* the loop trail follows power lines on to old road, crosses power lines again, and continues on old road through deep laurel. It crosses main trail at .56 m. *(North Crossover)* and overlooks ecology tower by Conn. River at .7 m. Loop returns to main trail at 1.06 m. *(Midway Junction)*, follows main trail for .11 m. and leaves at 1.17 m. *(Summit Junction)*. Loop trail crosses old stone wall and then reaches main trail at 1.75 m. *(South Crossover)*, and crosses it. Loop ends at *South Junction* with main trail at 2.21 m., 0.11 m. from Aircraft Rd. The whole trail abounds in blueberries in late June, early July.

RESERVOIR

The reservoir trail begins on Brooks Rd. near the Conn. Valley Hospital reservoir, gradually ascends with scenic views of reservoir. Trail departs from reservoir at .23 m., crosses wood road at .31

m., proceeds through open rocky outcropping with views of Middletown. Trail turns and crosses over loop trail, *Old Burn Crossing* at .52 m. Traversing brook, trail winds upwards over bluff, descends and turns at .72 m., crosses loop at *Twins Crossing* at .84 m. on Reservoir Rd. Crossing brook at .98 m. trail climbs steep ledge to overlook reservoirs at 1.06 m. with view of Powder Ridge. Trail terminates at Rockpile Cave, at 1.31 m.

Reservoir Loop

This loop trail begins at Rockpile Cave, intersects wood road at .32 m., follows along road and meets dirt extension of Reservoir Rd. at .41 m. At .52 m. the loop trail meets the main trail at *Twins Crossing*, crosses brook and crosses main trail, *Old Burn Crossing*, at .72 m., skirting the swamp at 1.17 m., and reaches reservoir at 1.27 m. Passing a quarry at 1.41 m., the trail follows around a swamp at 1.61 m. and ends at Brooks Rd. at 1.91 m.

Central Division

(Direction of travel: N to S as far as Broomstick Ledges, then E to W to Rt. 17, after which it is S to N.)

EAGLE'S BEAK POINT

(U.S.G.S. quadrangles: Durham, Haddam)

The Central Division starts on Brainard Hill Rd. in Haddam. From Rt. 9 take Exit 10 (Aircraft Rd.) to Saybrook Rd. (Rt. 154, formerly Rt. 9A), turn R and follow Saybrook Rd. .7 m. to Thayer Rd. (Seven Falls and Eastern Division here), turn R and follow Thayer Rd. .1 m. to Nedobity Rd., turn R and follow Nedobity Rd. .8 m. to Brainard Hill Rd., turn R and follow Brainard Hill Rd. 1 m. to trailhead.

From Brainard Hill Rd., cross dam and brook, gradually ascend through fine stand of mountain laurel to rocky outlook. Trail soon traverses "The Pavement" (a long flat slab of rock) and reaches Eagle's Beak Point at 1.07 m. with excellent view. The trail crosses a power line, then a brook, runs along top of ledges, descends gradually to a large brook and reaches Foothills Rd. at 2.5 m.

Cross Foothills Rd., follow private driveway

through backyard, gradually ascend to rocky outcrop, descend, cross brook and reach Wiese Albert Rd. at 3.33 m.

MILLER'S POND AND BEAR ROCK
(U.S.G.S. quadrangle: Durham)

From Wiese Albert Rd., trail gradually descends, partly on woods road, to Miller's Pond, an undeveloped State Park. Trail follows S and W shorelines to the dam at 4.09 m.

Trail turns sharp L and ascends ridge, crosses several brooks, climbs steeply, then more gradually along top of cliffs to rocky summit at 5.44 m. The excellent view extends SW, W to N with Durham's church spire in the center. The background, L to R, is: Bluff Hill, Pistapaug Mt., Fowler Mt., Trimountain, Reed Gap, Mt. Beseck, Mt. Higby and Mt. Lamentation.

The trail descends sharply, passing under the massive overhang of Bear Rock, crosses a woods road, then a telephone cableline and reaches Higganum Rd., at 6.35 m.

COGINCHAUG CAVE
(U.S.G.S. quadrangle: Durham)

From Higganum Rd., trail crosses brook, ascends rather steeply to ridge, descends past swampy area on L, ascends to rocky outcrop, descends and skirts top of cliffs to good W viewpoint. Trail descends to Coginchaug Cave at 7.3 m.

The trail turns L along base of cliff, ascends steeply to the ridge, descends, crosses several brooks, follows wood road and reaches end of paved road at 8.01 m. (Limited parking.) Follow paved Old Blue Hills Rd. to Rt. 79 at 8.6 m.

MT. PISGAH, MICA LEDGES, AND BROOMSTICK LEDGES
(U.S.G.S. quadrangle: Durham)

From Rt. 79 (.8 m. S of Rt. 17 in Durham) trail enters Sand Hill Rd. (W) and turns immediately L (S) onto Pisgah Rd. Trail follows Pisgah Rd. .25 m., turns R (W) and ascends on old trace at moderate grade. It continues uphill to gravel road and near top, turns R over ledge to summit of Mt. Pisgah (El. 644 ft.) at 1.16 m. with fine view of Coginchaug Valley, trap rock ridges to the W, Middletown and Hartford to the N, and Bluff Head to the SW.

Trail leaves summit toward the S, passes over ledge, descends on gravel road 100 yds., then swings R and descends steeply, bears R to Chalker Brook at 1.51 m. Trail crosses brook, turns L (S), follows brook 100 yds., turns R and ascends to Cream Pot Rd. (gravel) at 1.57 m. Trail crosses road, then follows wood road to Pyramid Rock at 1.78 m., ascends steeply to top of ridge at 2.05 m., (frequent W views of cultivated fields and trap rock ridges from the Mica Ledges). At 2.51 m., trail passes a pile of rocks which marks the corner of Durham, Guilford, and Madison with early survey dates. Trail descends steeply through gully, ascends over a ledge with a view at 2.74 m. Trail descends through hollow and then continues uphill on old trace to gravel road at 3.56 m. Trail turns R on wood road, then L on another wood road. It turns R off road at 4.04 m., then goes S through woods, partly on wood roads. It bears R (W) at 5.0 m. on a wood road, then winds partly on old trace and partly in woods around and over the Broomstick Ledges. It goes past bogs and a charcoal pit and then turns R, crossing brook at 6.0 m. It turns L then R around a large rock, turns R (N) past bog and ascends up ridge. It follows the ridge N and then descends steeply on W to Rt. 77 at 6.4 m.

BLUFF HEAD AND TOTOKET MOUNTAIN

(U.S.G.S. quadrangle: Durham)

From Rt. 77, trail goes along old road SW about 100 yds., turns sharp R and climbs steeply, skirting top of cliffs with numerous good views overlooking Myer Huber Pond, the Coginchaug Valley N to Durham and beyond, and S to Long Island Sound. Trail continues across a high plateau, then descends W through hemlock grove and crosses brook, crosses another high plateau and enters old woods rd. Trail turns R off woods rd. then turns L and descends steeply to ravine with interesting brook (sometimes dry). Trail swings W, then N through overgrown pasture to paved rd. (Stage Coach Rd.), which is followed W a few hundred yds. to Rt. 17 at 3.22 m. This point is .5 m. N of the Durham/North Branford town line. (New Haven 14 m. S, Middletown 12 m. N.)

PAUG AND TRIMOUNTAIN

(U.S.G.S. quadrangle: Durham)

Trail follows Rt. 17 R (N) .07 m., then goes W at small highway bridge, crosses brook then swings R (N) along brook for 100 yds., then L and ascends S on wood road to ridge of Pistapaug Mt., turns N and follows ridge to picturesque bluffs overlooking Pistapaug Pond. Trail continues N, swings W, and descends steep wood road to Paug Gap at 2.37 m. Trail crosses road and climbs Fowler Mt., with glimpses of Paug Pond. At top of ridge, trail turns N through undeveloped Trimountain State Park. At 4.17 m. trail crosses abandoned Wadsworth Farm Rd. (From Wallingford to Durham, used by Washington in 1775 and 1789).

Trail now passes under three notches to avoid exposure to firing range and ascends a steep slope of loose cobbles to an outlook. At 5.12 m. trail is relocated sharply E to avoid quarry operations. *N. H. T. R. quarry blasting warning is five long siren blasts five minutes before detonation.* Due to logging, trail may be lost for short distance, especially south-bound; search for blazes on W side of logging area.

Relocated trail follows a brook ravine, passing a small waterfall at 5.6 m. Bearing N from ravine, trail emerges on cleared S. N. E. T. right-of-way at 6.07 m., which it follows N to Rt. 68 just E of Gap Rd., which is followed .2 m. W to trail junction at 6.5 m. at Reed's Gap. (Wallingford 5.3 m. W, Durham 3 m. E)

BESECK

(U.S.G.S. quadrangles: Durham, Middletown)

Trail N crosses Air Line R.R. tracks to farm road. Follow road (which soon becomes a wood road) NW to lower end of Beseck ridge. (Beseck is corruption of Besett, Indian word for "black.") Trail follows cliffs over 7 promontories. Old Middlefield Mt. stage road is crossed just N of halfway point. Highest point on mountain is 840 ft. Trail skirts high cliffs overlooking Black Pond and descends to Rt. 66 .3 m. W of Rt. 147 at 5.7 m. (Meriden 3.9 m. W, Middletown 5.1 m. E.)

MOUNT HIGBY

(U.S.G.S. quadrangles: Middletown, Meriden)

New access trail (purple dot) from Guida's Dairy Bar on Rt. 66 travels .35 m. W to meet through trail. Park behind Guida's Dairy Bar.

Also limited parking and access where Rt. 66 becomes divided highway going W of where trail crosses Rt. 66, at Probus National sign. Climb approx. .1 m. N (unmarked) to L (W) turn and blue blazes.

From Rt. 66, trail ascends hillside NW, then swings W on wood road parallel to highway, at .4 m. turns R (N) and ascends steep ridge, and at 1 m. reaches The Pinnacle, the best viewpoint on Mt. Higby. The view extends almost 360 degrees from Mt. Tom, Mass. to Long Island Sound at New Haven. Trail runs close to cliff's glacial grooves 50 yds. N of Pinnacle, then descends to Preston Notch (water usually found here) at 1.7 m. Trail makes long climb to N part of Mt. Higby (892 ft.) Interesting natural bridge formation marked "N.B." is at this point. Trail continues along ridge, then descends NE at 2.5 m. Finally it bears L on woods rd to Country Club Rd., at 4.3 m. This point is the N end of the Central Division of the Mattabesett Trail. To continue N on the trail, turn L (N) and follow Country Club Rd. (crossing I-91 in .3 m.), continue W on Country Club Rd. about 2.2 m. to foot of Chauncey Peak.

Northern Division

CHAUNCEY PEAK AND LAMENTATION

(U.S.G.S. quadrangles: Meriden, Middletown)

From Meriden-Highland highway (Country Club Rd., in Middletown, Westfield Rd. in Meriden) 5 m. W of the Suzio Office and Quarry, trail ascends very steeply (hikers may disregard no trespassing signs) to summit of Chauncey Peak at .5 m., with excellent views. Trail skirts top of cliffs eastward, then circles L and follows ridge N. Trail soon overlooks picturesque Crescent Lake 400 feet below. At .77 m. the trail reaches the best viewpoint of the lake, then descends steeply to the canal at 1.8 m. (By following the E side of this canal about .3 m. a marker is reached which indicates the corner of three counties: Hartford,

New Haven, and Middlesex.) Trail crosses canal and ascends to the S end of Lamentation Mt. and a viewpoint at 1.76 m. Trail passes a U.S.G.S. marker (El. 720 ft.) at 2.12 m. This almost level ridge is perhaps the most scenic traprock ridge walk in the state. Trail enters a wood road at 3.21 m. and leaves it at 3.4 m. Trail then ascends to the rocky N summit at 3.7 m. and soon starts the long descent NE and reaches Stantack Rd. (old town road) at 4.37 m. Trail turns L (N) and follows Stantack Rd. to Spruce Brook Rd. at 4.84 m. (limited parking). This point is the N end of the Northern Division of the Mattabesett Trail. Wilbur Cross Highway Rt. 15 is .7 m. L (W) on Spruce Brook Rd. The Metacomet Trail starts on the W side of the Wilbur Cross Highway 200 ft. S of Spruce Brook Road.

MATTATUCK TRAIL

The Mattatuck Trail passes many beautiful lakes and streams and crosses two interesting mountains, Prospect and Mohawk. It is approximately 35 miles total. Mattatuck was the Indian name for the intervale between Waterville and Naugatuck. See Mattatuck Trail map.

BUTTERMILK FALLS

(U.S.G.S. quadrangles: Southington, Bristol, Thomaston)

Trailhead is on Mad River Rd. at intersection with Rt 69. in Wolcott (.1 m. N of Rt. 322) Trail follows road .1 m., turns R into Peterson Memorial Park, proceeds through parking lot, turns L into woods then R onto a wood road. Follow wood road crossing a brook at .4 m. Continue to Mad River at .6 m., pass through hemlock groves along the river, and an old dam at 1.3 m. Trail turns L at 1.4 m. through a small clearing, crossing power lines onto a wood road beside a brook. At 1.5 m. trail turns L (W) gradually ascending a hill and turning N onto wood road and descending to Spindle Hill Rd. at 1.9 m. (limited parking along road beyond trail). Turn L onto road, then R crossing road into woods. Continue, crossing a brook at 2.7 m., to Charlie Krug Cave at 2.8 m. Trail continues through woods, crossing a wood road and to a second wood road at 3.1 m. (Indian Jack Cave, so called because an Indian named Jack lived there with his family in the early nineteenth century, is .1 m. to L along wood road). Main trail heads R following wood road until it peters out and continues out of woods across a field, along private driveway to Allentown Rd. at 3.7 m. (Indian Heaven Pond is .1 m. R along road, parking to R across from pond). Trail crosses road through an overgrown field into woods to Hemlock Hill, descending to Hancock Brook near an old dam at 4.1 m. Cross brook (may require wading during high water), turn L and follow brook to Buttermilk Falls (Nature Conservancy Area) at 4.2 m. Follow brook partway down falls, then turn R through woods to Lane Hill Rd., turn L, descend hill, turn L at bottom to intersection of S. Main St. and S. Eagle Rd. at 4.6 m. (Parking on S. Main St. across from Lane Hill Rd.)

MOUNT TOBE

(U.S.G.S. quadrangle: Thomaston)

At road junction trail turns R onto S. Eagle Rd. over R.R. Bridge to wood road on L at .3 m *(No parking on wood road per owner's request)*. Trail follows wood road into woods, crosses brook at .6 m., continues to cross power line at 1 m. and onto a wood road. Turn L at 1.2 m., proceed to another wood road and turn L onto road and bear R at fork. Continue along, climbing a slab ridge and cross power lines at 1.6 m. (View to R (W) above power lines). Trail descends from ridge to a cross trail, turns R and bears L at fork proceeding to a picturesque brook at 1.9 m. Continue through woods criss-crossing brook and descend to Todd Hollow Rd. at 2 m. *(Note: next part of trail through Todd Hollow may be partially flooded at times.)* Turn L on road, proceed to Ed's Big Pebble, turn R across road and sand dunes to edge of brush. Trail turns R, continues onto wood road at 2.3 m., bears R at fork following brook bed, bears L at next two forks, climbing a hill into woods. Continue to cross brook, climb a hill, turn L and re-cross brook at 2.6 m. Trail proceeds through woods to cross power lines at 3.1 m., (Brophy Pond to L down hill) continues crossing side trails at 3.2 m and 3.5 m. Continue to cross rock slab (Lowrey's Lookout), descend to Mt. Tobe Rd. (Rt.

262) at 3.7 m. (limited parking). Turn L, proceed to Wilton Rd. at 3.9 m., turn R onto Wilton Rd., descend hill and cross bridge to Carter Rd. at 4.6 m. (Wilton Pond is to the R). Turn L on Carter Rd. to wood road, turn R, follow wood road to an old foundation at 4.9 m. Trail turns R, ascends Cedar Mt. to a view to W at 5.2 m. Crossing rock slab ridge with fine views to W of Naugatuck Valley, trail continues to edge of woods at 5.7 m. Turn L onto short length of gravel road and onto abandoned paved road, descend to West Hill Rd. at 5.9 m. Trail crosses road into woods, climbs a hill to view at 6.1 m., crosses a brook at 6.2 m., and descends to Thomaston Ave. (old Rt. 8) at 6.3 m. Turn R and continue across Reynolds Bridge at 6.4 m. (Parking on E side of River.)

MATTATUCK FOREST

(U.S.G.S. quadrangle: Thomaston)

From Reynolds Bridge turn S, take R fork (Reynolds Bridge Rd.). At crossroad continue S on water co. R.O.W. Turn L then R, follow W side of Branch Brook behind Envirite plant and sewage treatment plant. Cross concrete bridge, turn N along E side of Rt. 8 to highway bridge. Turn W under the bridge, continuing uphill along old quarry road past Reynolds Quarry, then S through a picturesque intervale. Ascend gradually to interesting Rock House and Jericho Trail junction, with Crane Lookout on R at 1.5 m. (Jericho Trail continues 3.5 m. to Frost Bridge.) Descend to small brook. Cross brook and continue to U.S. 6 at 2.4 m. Cross and go into woods to old U.S. 6 at Black Rock Park at 2.7 m. Cross highway and go past pond; climb to Black Rock at 3.5 m. Descend gradually to Northfield Rd. at 4.3 m.

WATERBURY RESERVOIRS AND BEAVER POND

(U.S.G.S. quadrangles: Thomaston and Litchfield)

From Northfield Rd. continue NW through Glen of Valkyries to Boiling Spring Register 1.1 m., crossing brook. Continue on, crossing dirt road, to White Oak Spring at 1.8 m., through pines to French Brook at 2.1 m. Follow ledges with occasional views of Waterbury Reservoirs to

Rt. 109 at 2.9 m. (East Morris L.) Cross highway and follow dirt town road with Morris Reservoir on right. Turn L at 3.1 m., cross brook, go up steep bank and along Goat Path, a narrow ridge, cross Farnham Rd. at 4.1 m., and continue to Slab Meadow Rd., a dirt town road, at 5.1 m. Cross road and follow trail W through woods to Beaver Pond at 5.9 m. Turn L (W) across cement dam to woods road of White Memorial Foundation and follow blazes, mostly on similar roads, past Heron Pond to Rt. 63 at 8.1 m. (Litchfield 2 m. right; Watertown 8.5 m., left).

PROSPECT MOUNTAIN

(U.S.G.S. quadrangles: Litchfield, New Preston, Cornwall)

Cross highway through picnic area, and continue on wood roads of White Foundation, pass Cranberry Pond, cross Webster Rd. (dirt), and continue through woods to paved road and highway bridge over Bantam River at 1.5 m. Trail crosses highway on dirt rd., turns R over truss bridge, then R again at stone gate posts. (White Memorial hdqtrs. and museum on L.) Follow wood roads to reach paved road again at 2.3 m. Turn R and follow road 100 yds. past entrance to White Foundation at Rt. 202. (Litchfield 2 m. R; Bantam 1 m. L). Trail is interrupted at this point for a distance of 13 m. to Flat Rocks Rd. The continuation may be reached by following roads in Litchfield through the village of Milton and continuing NW into Cornwall. From Flat Rocks Road go NE to College St.

MOHAWK MOUNTAIN

(U.S.G.S. quadrangle: Cornwall)

At College St. proceed L 100 ft., turn R (N) on abandoned road, cross road at 1 m. and follow Camp Mohawk Rd. to R turn at 1.4 m. then E to Mohawk Pond. Turn N paralleling the E shore of Mohawk Pond, then veer away from the pond and out to dirt road. Continue N along dirt forest road, and then turn back into woods to the summit of Mohawk Mt. (1680 ft.) at 2.9 m. Follow dirt road, then L on trail past camp grounds and springs to Clark's Hill to junction with the Mohawk Trail at 4.3 m.

METACOMET TRAIL

The Metacomet Trail in Connecticut follows the striking trap rock range running from the Hanging Hills of Meriden to the Massachusetts line for approximately 51 miles. It is named for the Indian, Metacomet (Prince Philip), who is supposed to have directed the burning of Simsbury from one of the summits. The trail continues across Massachusetts to Mt. Monadnock in New Hampshire. See three maps: Metacomet/Mattabesett; Metacomet—U.S. 6 to Tariffville; and Metacomet—North Section.

THE HANGING HILLS

(U.S.G.S. quadrangle: Meriden)

The trail begins on Rt. 15 (Berlin Turnpike) in Berlin, 200 yds. S of the northern Mattabesett Trail terminus on Spruce Brook Rd. Trail follows Orchard Rd., crosses Toll Gate Rd. at .2m., and leaves road, bearing S through gate at jct. of Orchard and Kensington Rd. at 1.6 m. Trail passes S of two ponds, through gate, and follows W side of Crooked Brook to power line at 2.8 m. Trail turns R, following power line NW, and crosses development road at 3.0 m. A few yards after crossing rd., trail turns L and follows a right of way between houses and then a rd. bearing SW. It crosses development rd. at 4.1 m. and then crosses brook and Rt. 71 (Chamberlain Hgwy.) at 5.0 m.

Trail follows an old path and passes over Elmere Reservoir Dam at 5.2 m., continues to N end of Merimere Reservoir at 6.1 m. with a fine view of lake and notch from the dam. Trail follows W bank of the reservoir, emerging on cliffs opposite Mine Island. Trail reaches Castle Craig, the lookout tower on East Peak at 7.2 m. (An auto road from Meriden also goes to summit.) Trail descends to lower road and climbs picturesque gorge to West Peak at 8.4 m.

Note pillow structure of first layer of lava and closer texture of last 500 ft.; surface of summit has been polished by glacial action. The view from West Peak (1024 ft.) is one of the finest in Connecticut.

From West Peak trail crosses a power line, goes N on wooded ridge. At 10.2 m. trail turns L, descends talus slope bearing W, crosses power line and reaches Rt. 364 at 10.8 m. [Here Rt. 364 is Kensington Rd. in Southington. About 0.4 m. east it becomes Southington Rd. in Kensington.] Trail follows Rt. 364 NE about a mile to Edgewood Rd. Total distance from Rt. 15: about 12 m.

RAGGED MOUNTAIN

(U.S.G.S. quadrangles: Meriden, New Britain)

On this section, be on the lookout for copperheads. Trail turns L on Southington Rd. (Rt. 364) for 120 yds., bears R along powerline to Edgewood Rd., turns L to Rt. 364 to highway trail sign, then turns sharply R into woods along Berlin Golf Course, descending L across brook at .3 m. and at .5 m. swings sharply L over loose rock (many spring wildflowers here) to E ridge of Little Mt., reaching S outlook with good views at .7 m. Trail follows cliffs, descending by narrow ledge, turns N at .7 m., crosses small stream and continues via road to Hart's Pond Rd., at .8 m.

Trail follows road W 100 yds. to edge of orchard. It turns R passing through orchard N toward cliff and climbs steeply through draw on W side of rock climbing area to excellent view at 1.1 m. Continuing N and W trail reaches summit of Ragged Mt. (761 ft.) at 1.5 m. with superb view. (From either end of this trap rock cliff unmarked trails may be followed to a series of caves formed by huge inclined slabs fallen away from the base of the outcrop. This entire area is fine practice ground for rock climbing.)

Trail continues N along edge of summit and turns sharp R descending E, then swinging NW, crosses several ravines toward remaining ridge at 2.2 m. and descends by wood road to R turn at 2.4 m. into Lost Valley. There the trail skirts the edge of Wesel Reservoir past overlook along steep ledge, and descends steeply L along bottom of cliff. Trail turns R at base of dam, then passes through woods to top of dam.

At 3.5 m. trail winds up ledge for ascent of ridge to NW, turns back along cliffs, swings W through woods and picks up old trail in 200 yards. Passing a S outlook, the trail reaches NW cliffs at 3.7 m. Crossing power line with beautiful views along way, it continues NE to Shuttle

Meadow Reservoir at 4.9 m. [This portion of the trail is part of the National Park Environmental Study Area.] Trail follows road E to canal at 5.1 m. and then goes N on canal and power line to road bordering reservoir on NE at 5.6 m. It turns L (W) on road, passing dam at 6 m. and reaches gate on reservoir property at 6.1 m. *No parking on water company roads.*

BRADLEY MOUNTAIN

(U.S.G.S. quadrangle: New Britain)

From gateway N of Shuttle Meadow Reservoir, trail threads NW through interesting boulder-strewn land. Crossing several ravines, it works W to big rock at .5 m. and then N. A good W outlook is reached at .8 m. It crosses power line and turns W again with outlooks at 1.5 m. and again at 1.7 m. Traveling N, trail ascends sharply to summit of Bradley Mt. (685 ft.) at 1.9 m.

Trail continues N over a series of rock summits with views near Sunset Rock Park (undeveloped) turns L (W) to Ledge Rd. Trail follows Ledge Rd., crosses Woodford Ave., I-84, and reaches Rt. 372 at 3.05 m. (New Britain 3 m. E, Plainville, 1.8 m. W).

RATTLESNAKE MOUNTAIN

(U.S.G.S. quadrangles: New Britain, Avon)

Trail turns R near Getty station, continues E on road .25 m. to large rock. Trail turns L (N) through small field and over loose rock to Pinnacle Rock at 2 m. with remarkable view. A rocky point overlooks "the straits," a narrow valley under SE cliffs of Rattlesnake Mt. at 3 m. Trail descends into the straits to wood road (leading to U.S. 6, useful for round trip walk over Rattlesnake Mt.) After a few hundred feet, trail leaves wood road by sharp L turn and climbs steeply to South Rattlesnake, with fine views. Swinging W, trail reaches Bill Warren's Den, a picturesque jumble of great boulders, at 3.5 m. [Said Warren, according to tradition, after being flogged for not going to church, tried to burn the village of Farmington, and was pursued into the mountains, where some Indian squaws hid him in this spot.]

Trail turns W, descends Rattlesnake Mt. to orchard, swings to N and E past TV tower anchor, skirts access road and emerges on paved road just S of U.S. 6 at 4 m. *Hikers should not park cars on TV company's road.*

Trail crosses U.S. 6 at rock cut, climbs ridge and continues NE to Poplar Hill Dr. It follows road to Mountain Rd. at 5 m. At 5.2 m. trail enters woods and continues to highway fence at 5.5 m. Trail continues through opening in fence, crosses intersection at traffic light, and continues on W side of Rt. 4 (Farmington Ave.) to Pratling Pond Rd.

TALCOTT MOUNTAIN

(U.S.G.S. quadrangle: Avon)

Starting at Farmington Ave., Rt. 4, (1 m. E of Farmington) trail goes N on Pratling Pond Rd. At .4 m. trail bears R on wood road. At 1.1 m. wood road reaches Metacomet Rd. Trail follows this road for a short distance and bears L to follow old trail to intersection with Talcott Notch Rd. At 1.4 m. trail crosses road and power line, then follows wood road to Old Mtn. Rd. at 1.9 m. Trail turns L (W) up hill and then R on wood road, which is followed to power line at 2.2 m. Trail follows path along power line (no trail markers) to Metropolitan District road at 2.5 m. It turns L uphill and enters woods at 2.6 m. After 0.1 m. through the woods, trail crosses M.D.C. road and then continues to Kilkenny Rock at 2.7 m.

Trail follows M.D.C. road, passes road on R at 2.9 m., enters woods at 3.3 m., and continues to power line clearing at 3.4 m. It crosses power line and reenters woods, turning L at 3.6 m. and L again at 3.7 m. Trail joins E-W wood road at 4.1 m., turns R off road at 4.2 m. and follows ledge. Leaving ledge, trail descends to power line and stream at 5 m., crosses stream, turns R and joins wood road. It turns L on M.D.C. road at 5.2 m. and continues to Albany Ave. (U.S. 44) at 5.8 m. (5.5 m. W of Hartford. Parking at main entrance to Reservoir 6, N of Albany Ave.)

From Albany Ave., at M.D.C. gate, just beyond main entrance to Reservoir 6, trail crosses highway, goes N into woods and follows viaduct to M.D.C. road at 6 m. Trail continues along W shore of reservoir. At 7.7 m. trail crosses bridge at N end of reservoir and continues N on wood road to crossroads at 8.1 m. (Side trail to W leads to Heublein Tower.) Trail continues N and soon crosses utility right-of-way, continues to powerline at 8.4 m., passes chimney ruins on R at 8.6 m., turns E at 8.8. m. crossing powerline again at 8.9 m. Trail turns N and reaches Rt. 185 just opposite entrance to Penwood State Park at 9.3 m. (7 m. NW of Hartford).

PENWOOD TO TARIFFVILLE

(U.S.G.S. quadrangles: Avon, Tariffville)

From Rt. 185 hikers enter Penwood State Park. A bronze tablet at the Park entrance is inscribed "Penwood, Donated to the people of Connecticut as a State Park by Curtis H. Veeder, a great lover of nature, 1944." The Park is beautifully forested with mature growths of hemlock and hardwoods. Rocks and glacial erratics of the trap ridge are of considerable interest to geologists. Wild flowers, ferns, and other ground growths abound. There are various side trails and old roads within the Park.

Entering the Park from Rt. 185, the trail follows the hard surfaced Park Rd. to the R. After turning L from rd. at .2 m., it ascends to trap ridge at .4 m. Trail continues N along ridge and descends into sag at .7 m. (Panorama Point Trail leads L 150 ft. to high point on ridge with good view W over the Farmington River Valley.)

Main trail continues N through hemlock and hardwood forest, and enters wood road. (At 1.1 m. there is a path leading L to Park Rd. in 100 yds.) Trail follows wood road to the R, and shortly thereafter turns L, ascending through thick growth of mountain laurel. Trail descends gradually through large hemlocks, passing stone pedestal on R at 1.7 m. It descends along wide graded path to N limit of Park Rd. at Lake Louise at 1.8 m. It turns L on grass-grown road along N shore of lake. At 2 m. trail turns R up stone steps and passes lookout site with fine views. [Alternate trail (blue blazes with red dots) continues straight ahead for about .2 m. before turning R (NE) and ascending the ridge to rejoin the main trail at ridgetop.] The trail continues N along the ridge to good viewpoint marked by iron pin at 3.1 m. From there it descends steeply to dead end of hard-surfaced Wintonbury Rd. and N end of State Park at 3.3 m. (Wintonbury Rd. leads L .5 m. to Terry's Plain Rd., Simsbury.)

After crossing Wintonbury Rd., the trail ascends through cedars, then gradually climbs the trap ridge to fine viewpoint at 3.8 m. Beyond, trail crosses several rocky knobs and power lines at 4.1 m., 4.4 m. and 4.9 m. Ruins of the Bartlett tower, a relic of a former recreational development, are passed at 5.3 m. The trail descends along abandoned carriage road to Mountain Rd., which leads L downhill to Rt. 189 in Tariffville at 5.9 m.

TARIFFVILLE TO PHELPS ROAD, SUFFIELD

(U.S.G.S. quadrangles: Tariffville, Windsor Locks, West Springfield, Mass.)

Because of highway changes, this part of the trail now starts at end of Tunxis Ave. This point is reached by taking the first R turn N of the Farmington River on Rt. 187, proceeding S on South Main St., East Granby, to the Farmington River and then W on Tunxis Ave. along the river to end of road.

Starting from Tunxis Avenue, on the N side of the Farmington River, the Blue Trail leads up a steep, rocky slope to a fine lookout at .2 m. Continuing E and N through a hemlock grove, the trail reaches an open ledge at 1.3 m. with extensive views to the W and S. From there, the trail descends on an old farm road N to Hatchett Hill Rd. at 1.4 m.

Two hundred feet W on Hatchett Hill Rd., the trail climbs a steep slope to the R, crossing under a power line. At the top the trail turns N across a stone wall and continues through scattered red cedars to a grove of white pines at 1.8 m. (This is the site of an 18th century cemetery where smallpox victims were buried. Vandals have removed headstones until there is not one left.) The peak at 1.9 m. affords good views.

The trail continues along the crest for some distance, then turns and descends the E slope to a large white oak. Northward through a one-time pasture, the trail reaches the edge of thick woods at 2.3 m., where old wood roads diverge in several directions. The trail follows one N, crossing an abandoned R.R. line and climbs a steep slope through woods to a fence line which is followed up along the ridge and descends on the N slope to Holcomb St. at 2.9 m. *When passing the large rock quarry, a special effort should be made to keep strictly on the marked trail.*

Following Holcomb St. N to its junction with Rt. 20 and continuing about 100 yards N on Newgate Rd., the trail enters the woods and travels N and E to the top of the ridge at 3 m. The trail then leads N along the crest with good views E and W. Continuing N through deciduous woods to Peak Mt. (672 ft.) at 3.9 m., the highest point on the range between Tariffville and the Massachusetts Line. Trail descends Peak Mt. on the N to a col at 4 m. (A side trail (unmarked) leads down the western slope to Newgate Prison.)

From the Newgate connection, the trail continues N along the crest through a hardwood forest to Turkey Hills Lookout at 4.2 m. with distant views W. The trail continues N through a grove of red cedars. At the N edge of this grove the trail crosses the East Granby-Suffield town line and ascends a slope to the edge of a ravine which was traditionally used by the Indians as a trail over the mountain. The trail descends into this ravine and climbs the steep N slope to a trap rock crag of Chimney Point at 5 m. with good views S and W. At 5.6 m. trail enters the property of Suffield Conservancy and town park. Trail runs N along trap rock ridge, then E to a wood rd. It continues N on wood rd., then turns E and goes down a steep slope to Phelps Rd.

From this point, it is necessary to follow blacktopped roads to pick up the continuation N of the Metacomet in Mass. The route follows Phelps Rd. E to Mountain Rd. (Rt. 168) at 6.9 m., and turns L (N) on Mountain Rd. to Warnertown Rd. at 7.9 m. It continues N on Warnertown Rd. to S. Longyard Rd. at 7.9 m. and crosses the Conn.-Mass. State Line at 8.9 m. It goes R (E), past North Stone St. at 9.3 m. The trail N passes just E of Harts Pond on Barry St. The Metacomet Trail in Massachusetts begins here.

MOHAWK TRAIL

(U.S.G.S. quadrangles: Cornwall, Ellsworth, South Canaan)

The 25-mile Mohawk Trail was established as a blue-blazed hiking trail on May 8, 1988. It follows the former "Eastern" or traditional route of the Appalachian Trail, which was not needed after a new route was opened through Sharon from Route 4 to Falls Village.

Two recent events have had a significant negative impact on the new trail. The first of them was the closing of the trail between Echo Rock and Valley Rd. in the fall of 1988. Then damage to the Cathedral Pines area by a tornado on July 10, 1989 effectively closed the trail there. Efforts are being made to reopen these parts of the trail and to improve its quality, while retaining it in this edition of *The Walk Book.*

APPALACHIAN TRAIL TO CORNWALL BRIDGE

0.0	The Mohawk trail starts where the Appalachian Trail crosses Old Sharon Rd., 0.2 m. N of Rt. 4. It goes E on Old Sharon Rd. and then goes L up an embankment.
0.5	After trail crosses Rt. 7 at a *parking area,* it crosses the Housatonic River on concrete highway bridge.
0.8	In village of Cornwall Bridge the trail reaches grassy triangle at intersection of Rts. 4 and 7. *(Parking on Rt. 4.)*

CORNWALL BRIDGE TO ECHO ROCK

0.0	From E side of grassy triangle at intersection of Rts. 4 and 7 *(parking on Rt. 4),* the trail follows paved Dark Entry Rd.
0.9	Trail crosses Bonnie Brook and then passes dam.
1.5	Trail crosses Brook again, in Dudleytown, an abandoned community.
2.5	Echo Rock (1,450 ft.) on side of Coltsfoot Mtn.—views of Cornwall Valley.

TRAIL ENDS HERE TEMPORARILY
It is closed from Echo Rock to beyond Cathedral Pines, a distance of a little over 3 m.

ESSEX HILL RD TO BUNKER HILL

0.0 Trail resumes beyond Cathedral Pines, going W on Essex Hill Rd.

0.2	Trail crosses Great Hill Rd. and follows driveway of private home into Mohawk State Forest.
1.1	Trail passes northern terminus of Mattatuck Trail. (1.4 m. S to summit of Mohawk Mtn.)
1.2	Trail crosses upper terminal of ski lift—good views.
1.4	Trail crosses Toumey Rd. *Camping Zone 9* (lean-to) is just beyond.
2.6	*Camping Zone 8* (lean-to).
2.7	Rt. 4 at top of Bunker Hill.

BUNKER HILL TO DEAN'S RAVINE

0.0	After crossing to N side of Rt. 4, trail continues to Red Mtn. Lean-to *(Camping Zone 7)*.
0.6	Trail reaches summit of Red Mtn. (1,653 ft.)
1.2	Trail turns R on Rt. 4 and follows it a short distance to "Four Corners" (Jct. Rts. 4 and 43.) There it turns R on Rt. 43.
3.2	Trail turns L into "Indian Lane."
4.9	Trail crosses Lake Rd.
6.5	Trail crosses dirt Ford Hill Rd. *(No parking.)*
8.2	Trail passes wildlife pond. Then in next 1.5 m. it crosses three State Forest rds.
10.4	Trail follows Wickwire Rd. to Pine Knoll Lean-to. *(Camping Zone 6*—unreliable spring.)
11.5	Trail reaches Music Mtn. Rd. and Dean's Ravine picnic area.

DEAN'S RAVINE TO IRON BRIDGE

0.0	From Dean's Ravine picnic area trail follows brook downstream.
0.5	Trail turns L from brook and R on Music Mtn. Rd.
0.6	Trail turns R and climbs enbankment into woods.
1.9	Trail reaches open ledges of "Lookout Point".
2.2	Summit of Barrack Mtn. (North Rock, 1,230 ft.)—Excellent views.
2.5	After very steep descent, trail crosses Rt. 7.
2.6	Trail crosses RR tracks and turns R on

paved Warren Tpk. (This is juction with the A.T. coming N on Warren Tpk. from Rt. 7 bridge. From here to the "Iron Bridge" the two trails follow same route.)

4.7 "Iron Bridge" across the Housatonic: terminus of Mohawk Trail.

MUIR TRAIL

(U.S.G.S. quadrangles: Torrington and West Torrington)

The John Muir Trail is located in Torrington. It runs NE from Sunny Brook State Park through Paugnut State Forest to Burr Pond State Park. See map John Muir Trail.

The trail begins at Sunny Brook Park parking area, on W side of Newfield Rd. about 3 m. N of Rt. 4 and Main St. It ascends through an impressive forest to mountain terrain (Walnut Mtn.) of ledges and boulders. (A side trail leads to the summit.) Then the trail passes over gently rolling terrain, through a mixed forest, and descends to Burr Road at about 4 m.

NARRAGANSETT TRAIL

The Narragansett Trail in Connecticut is substantially a wooded trail with views of the Atlantic and other geographical features from its high points. It follows and crosses several brooks, traverses wild ravines, and passes along five ponds or lakes in Connecticut and more in Rhode Island. The Connecticut portion described herein in three sections is 16 miles long. A fourth section describes an additional 4 miles in Rhode Island. See map Pequot Trail, Narragansett Trail.

LANTERN HILL TO GALLUP POND

(U.S.G.S. quadrangle: Old Mystic)

This section begins on Rt. 2 and ends where Rts. 2 and 201 join. On Rt. 2 (8 m. E of Norwich, 2.5 m. E of Rt. 164, and 4.5 m. NW of North Stonington) go S on Wintechog Rd. for .2 m. where trail leaves road R. At .4 m., pass end of Pequot Trail which joins from the R. Resume ascent through laurel to summit of Lantern Hill at .7 m. where one can see Block Island, Fishers Island, Montauk Point, Norwich, etc. Silex mine quarry nearby will eventually follow a vein through this summit. Descending S, trail passes through woods and laurel to Wintechog Rd. at 1.3 m. (Road L returns to trail in .6 m.) Following wood road through laurel, trail bears L at 1.5 m. At height of land trail bears L again, passing N of tower and follows old stone boundary. At 2.8 m. trail comes out of the S end of a field. It follows the S border to Gallup Pond dam at 2.9 m. After crossing dam, trail reaches Rts. 2 & 201 junction at 3 m. (Trail began on Rt. 2, 2.3 m. L; North Stonington is 2.3 m. R.)

GALLUP POND TO ROUTE 49

(U.S.G.S. quadrangles: Old Mystic, Ashaway, R.I., Voluntown)

After crossing Rts. 2 and 201, the trail follows Ryder Rd. for .1 m. and turns L into woods. At .5 m. there is a beautiful view across the Shunock River Valley to the ocean. Trail continues through the woods into hemlocks where it descends to Yawbux Brook. At 1.5 m. it crosses a dammed pond and open area established by the state for wildlife conservation. Trail follows brook to road at 2.7 m. (Road R leads .3 m. to Wyassup Lake Rd.; 3.3 m. to North Stonington P.O.) Follow road L past the Wyassup Lake boat launching area and parking lot. At 3.2 m. turn L onto wood road. At 3.4 m. continue straight, off the wood road, to High Ledge at 3.9 m. with fine view across Lake Wyassup to Westerly and the ocean. (At height of land, trail L leads to *lean-to*). At 4.6 m. turn R onto wood road. (Billings Lake .6 m. L) At 5 m. turn L onto another wood road. Descend to spring on L at 5.2 m. (At summit of short rough climb, 5.3 m., side trail R leads 50 ft. to Bullet Ledge viewpoint.) Trail continues to wood road crossing at 5.9 m. (Camp Wightman Rd. .8 m. to L.) At 6.5 m. in deep wooded hollow reach Myron Kinney Brook and follow upstream. Turn L onto wood road at 7 m. and Rt. 49 at 7.4 m. (Voluntown at Rt. 165 L 5.1 m.; Rt. 184 R 5.7 m.)

ROUTE 49 TO STATE LINE

(U.S.G.S. quadrangle: Voluntown)

After crossing Rt. 49 follow an abandoned right-of-way between pastures to abandoned house

NARRAGANSETT TRAIL 47

site at .3 m. (*From here to next blacktop road, the owner has requested that hikers stay strictly on the trail.*) Trail passes through woods along a series of old wood roads, across an earthen dam to sawmill at .8 m. Turn L. At 1.1 m., turn L onto blacktop road; at 1.3 m. R into woods. Pass fine spring 100 yds. from the road. Trail passes through woods, descends a small ravine, and alternately passes ledges and crosses three cascading brooks which may be dry in summer. Enter dirt Green Fall Rd. at 2.7 m. and descend to Green Fall River at 2.8 m. Follow river upstream through a beautiful hemlock wooded ravine to Green Fall Pond at the dam at 3.2 m. Trail crosses the dam and follows the shoreline to the R. (An alternate route blazed in orange and .5 m. longer follows the L shore, and passes through picnic and camping areas and by the terminus of the Nehantic Trail, all accessible by car.) At 3.9 m. where alternate route rejoins the trail, turn R from the shore into woods. At 4 m. go R onto wood road; at 4.1 m., L into woods. Pass peg mill site at 4.2 m., then through blueberry bush area to blue-blazed side trail at 4.7 m. (Side trail leads .1 m. L onto exposed rock with views across marsh.) Continue to Conn. State Line where at 4.9 m. a yellow blazed trail enters from L. (Yellow blazes denote trails in R.I.) Follow State Line S above huge rock cave to dirt Green Fall Rd. where Conn. portion of trail ends at 5.4 m. (Rt. 49 is 2.7 m. R.)

RHODE ISLAND SECTION
STATE LINE TO ASHVILLE POND

(U.S.G.S. quadrangle: Voluntown)

The trail, now blazed yellow, follows road L .2 m., where it turns R onto trail. (Trail ahead leads to Camp Yawgoog, R.I. in .7 m.) Trail soon follows W shore of Yawgoog Pond and then ascends to junction at 1.5 m. (Southern terminus of Tippecansett Trail). Bear R and at 1.8 m. turn L onto dirt Rockville Rd. Turn R from road at 2.1 m. and ascend gradually to high point with views R over Ell Pond and L over Long Pond. Descend cleft in rock formation, cross wet area and pass huge hemlocks in rough terrain to prominent view over Long Pond at 2.6 m. At 3.1 m. turn R onto wood road for a few yards, then L into woods. (Wood road in opposite direction leads to dirt Canonchet Rd. shortly.) At 3.8 m., after passing W end of Ashville Pond, trail turns L onto dirt road. Follow road to Canonchet Rd. at 4.3 m. (Highway R leads to R.I. Rt. 3 in 1.3 m.) (See *Mass. and R.I. Trail Guide. A.M.C.*)

NATCHAUG TRAIL

The Natchaug Trail traverses the James L. Goodwin and Natchaug State Forests between U.S. 6 in Hampton and the Nipmuck Trail in Westford for a distance of over 18 miles. See Maps #1 and #2 Natchaug Trail.

JAMES L. GOODWIN STATE FOREST

(U.S.G.S. quadrangle: Hampton)

From the James L. Goodwin Conservation Center, leave N edge of field below the parking lot. Skirt side of Pine Acres Lake, then cross old R.R. bed at .53 m. and reach Eleventh Section Rd. at .83 m. Follow road N for short distance, then enter red pine stand. Follow trail to Jones Rd. at 1.09 m. Turn L on road briefly, then R into white pine stand. After crossing several stone walls, trail enters tree-girdling demonstration area. At 1.27 m. trail turns N on old tote road and comes to Black Spruce Pond dam at 2.09 m. (Note: good bird-watching here.) Continue to the NW along top of dam, turn N with view of pond through mixed hardwoods, at 2.64 m. turn R onto old tote road. At 2.69 m. cross intersection with second forest road (Bartlett Rd.) Continue N, cross brook, and come out onto Eleventh Section Rd. (unpaved here). Go R less than .1 m., then turn L onto woods road through red pine stand. Leave woods road, pass through red pine stand. Leave woods road, pass through spruce stand, and then white pines, onto old tote road. Follow this road northerly to Orchard Hill at 3.46 m.

SOUTHERN NATCHAUG STATE FOREST

(U.S.G.S. quadrangle: Hampton)

Follow trail W. At .24 m. bear L to top of hill for outlook over valley. From lookout, follow trail N, crossing small brook and coming to Marcy Rd. at .86 m. Cross blacktop and continue through hardwoods. Cross Morey Rd. at 1.09 m. Descend to Goodwin Brook and proceed to feeder brook. When ground levels, follow trail R to old tote road, go L across brook, then R through mixed hardwoods, and L through small spruce stand. After crossing an old woods road, a spring can be found just off the trail to the L at 2.10 m. Proceed to state forest road at 2.25 m. (Note: following this forest road L will bring you out on Morey Rd., and L again completes circle, a walk of just over 2 m.)

Crossing state forest road, proceed into forest and cross pipe line right-of-way at 2.58 m. (A short walk L along pipe line to view over the Natchaug River valley.) Continue on trail to Beaverdam Brook at 2.98 m. Follow brook upstream to base of old milldam. Cross brook here and proceed to forest road (Kingsbury Rd.) at 3.25 m. Cross Kingsbury Rd., proceeding on dirt road to Beaver Meadow Marsh area at 3.34 m.

NORTHERN NATCHAUG FOREST

(U.S.G.S. quadrangles: Hampton, Eastford)

Leaving parking area at Beaver Meadow Marsh, follow trail N along W side of pond. After leaving pond and passing through several stands of spruces, regain Kingsbury Rd. at .58 m. Go R on blacktop .13 m., cross brook, and enter L into woods, coming onto the General Nathaniel Lyon Memorial Park picnic area at .83 m. (Parking; picnicking.) From Lyon Memorial Park, pick up trail on old tote road at NW corner of field. At 1.03 m., continue straight on trail to another tote road at 1.49 m. Follow L for short distance, enter woods, then parallel stone wall along slope which overlooks Natchaug valley. Note spectacular chestnut "skeleton," 15 ft. 6 in. circumference, at 1.91 m. After continuing another .37 m., and crossing two small brooks, enter an area with stones curiously heaped in a generally circular layout. Turn L at 2.58 m. on an old tote road. (R to Pilfershire Rd. in .13 m.)

Follow tote road downhill a few hundred feet, then turn R into woods. The trail descends to the bank of the Still River, and then follows the river N through an area with many beautiful large trees, reaching Pilfershire Rd. at 3.3 m. Turning L on this road, the trail immediately crosses the

Still River and shortly reaches General Lyon Rd. (Limited parking) Trail turns L, again staying on the road, to reach Rt. 198 at 3.4 m.

ROUTE 198 TO WESTFORD

(U.S.G.S. quadrangles: Hampton, Eastford, Westford)

Follow General Lyon Rd. S and continue S on Rt. 198. At .4 m., shortly after crossing the bridge over Bigelow Brook, turn R (W) down embankment and cross overgrown field to wood road. Turn R (N) on wood road and follow a short distance, then turn R (N) and climb incline. Continue through woods to a wood road and turn L (NW) up the road to a field. Cross field, then cross the river on a foot bridge. The trail then turns L (W) and climbs ridge, overlooking the river and follows the ridge, coming out in a small field. Keep to the R of field, cross a wood road and continue through woods. When wood road is reached turn L (N) and continue to U.S. 44 at 1.96 m.

Crossing U.S. 44 the trail enters woods a short distance W of Bigelow Brook. Turn L at stone wall and a short distance later turn R (NW) to Bigelow Brook. The trail then intermittently follows and leaves the brook in the next mile. The trail then descends to the brook at 3.96 m. *(Note: The trail is closed from this point to Moon Rd. between Oct. 1 and Feb. 1.)* Follow brook N until it reaches Ashford Rd. (also called North Rd.) at 4.39 m.

Turn L (W) on Ashford Rd. and then turn R at 4.52 m. (NW) up a wood road. At 4.9 m. turn sharp L (W) up another wood road and at 5.08 m. turn R (N) through barways. *(Replace bars.)* After crossing the second barway, bear L and at 5.56 m. pass a side trail R (N). At 6 m. turn L (NW) up a wood road and go to its end at field. Turn R (N) and follow trail to pasture. Go around stone wall and then over it. Go through woods to Moon Rd. at 6.5 m.

The trail follows Moon Rd. and enters State Forest, continuing until reaching a wood road at 6.96 m. Turn R (N) up the wood road and follow past a wildlife pond and stand of pines. Continue until T in wood road is reached at maze of stone walls and old cellars, and turn L (NW) up this wood road. Follow a short distance and then turn L (W) off wood road at 7.53 m. Following through woods and using parts of old wood road, join the Nipmuck Trail at 8.24 m. (Eastford-Westford Road is to the R (N) .61 m. on the Nipmuck Trail.)

NAUGATUCK TRAIL

(U.S.G.S. quandrangle: Naugatuck)

From Beacon Rd., Rt. 42, (1.1 m. from Rt. 63) the trail leads N and climbs by wood road and path 1 m. to a trail junction. (Side trail leads .3 m. to Beacon Cap, a glacial boulder with fine view in all directions.) From the junction the main trail goes W along the range and at 1.5 m. a rocky outcrop affords excellent views to the W. At 1.8 m. trail reaches second junction. (Side trail leads L to Rt. 42, about 1.5 m. from Rt. 63.)

The main trail continues down through a rocky gorge and reaches another intersection at 2.3 m. To the R the main trail continues NW through woods, crosses a utility line, passes an old orchard and a small pond and into woods again reaching a junction at 4.2 m. (Side trail leads .2 m. to Spruce Knoll with a good view into the Naugatuck Valley.) From this junction the main trail leads SW and drops to Rt. 8 (northbound lane) at 4.8 m. at the point where Egypt Brook empties into the Naugatuck River (1.7 m. N of the Naugatuck River Bridge at Beacon Falls).

To reach trailhead at Egypt Brook, leave Rt. 8 at the Cross St. exit. Cross Beacon Valley Brook on a small bridge just E of the highway and park in front of a chain link fence. Then walk S on dirt rd., which parallels Rt. 8, to the trailhead. See map Trails North of New Haven.

NAYANTAQUIT TRAIL

(U.S.G.S. quadrangle: Hamburg)

Nayantaquit was the name of an Indian tribe whose hunting grounds extended from what is now Rhode Island to the Connecticut River and

N to the grounds of the Nipmucks and Quinebaugs. The word probably means "point of land on a tidal river". The trail is located in the western section of the Nehantic State Forest in the town of Lyme. See map Nayantaquit Trail.

The Nayantaquit Trail consists of a single loop that is bisected by the N-S crossover and an access trail from Uncas Pond. It starts near the NE corner of the state forest at the parking lot. (Ample parking.) The parking lot may be reached by entering the park off Rt. 156 and driving NE past Uncas and Norwich Ponds, descending, and turning N around a gravel pit. The parking lot is L on a wood road. It can also be reached from the N by Keeny Rd. which turns S off Beaver Brook Rd. and becomes the park road on entering the park. Beaver Brook Rd. runs between Grassy Hill Rd. and Rt. 156. The parking lot is on the R a few hundred yds. after entering the park.

The Nayantaquit Trail goes SE from the parking lot and proceeds to a trail junction in about 300 yds. From this point the trail can be walked clockwise or counter clockwise. The full circle distance is 2.85 m. with the N-S crossover and access trail from Uncas Lake adding another .5 m. each.

		Miles
1.	Parking Lot	.00
	Pass boulder on L (looks like a chipmunk looking from the S)	
2.	East Junction. Proceed S	.15
3.	High Point	.42
	Continue towards Brown Hill	
4.	Brown Hill Junction	.79

The N-S crossover leaves from here heading N to the main loop (point 8) in .51 m. It passes numerous stone walls and former pastures.

Continuing S 1500 yds. we see several home foundations, a well, numerous stone walls, and junction with access trail from Uncas Pond.

Access trail E reaches the park road access from Uncas Pond in .53 miles. This trail joins a wood path for a short distance and then climbs up a short but steep rocky slope before descending to the road.

Continuing towards Nickerson Hill

proceed partly on a wood road and down a hill and across a bridge to a N-S wood road. Turn N here.

5.	Wood road turn off Turn W up wooded slope	1.35
6.	Summit Nickerson Hill (452 ft.) Continuing E pass some ledges with good views to the SE.	1.63
7.	North Junction Trail to E joins a wood road in a few hundred yds. Wood road goes E to parking lot. Continue on trail E past a stream flowing N.	2.07
8.	N-S Crossover Junction Continue to parking area via E junction.	2.34
2.	East Junction	2.70
1.	Parking Lot	2.85

NEHANTIC TRAIL

The Nehantic Trail extends from Green Fall Pond to Hopeville Pond State Park, going over ledges, Mt. Misery and Stone Hill, crossing brooks and skirting ponds. Total mileage about 14 miles. See map Nehantic Trail, Pachaug Trail.

GREEN FALL POND ROAD TO ROUTES 165 AND 138

(U.S.G.S. quadrangle: Voluntown)

The trail starts at Green Fall Pond near the camping area where the Pachaug Trail also originates and continues N and crosses brook. At .3 m. it crosses gravel road and another brook before ascending a ledge at 1.7 m. Trail crosses top and descends to wood road at 1.9 m., then bears N through evergreens and crosses gravel road at 3.3 m. (Fish Road, Rt. 49, is 1 m. W). Here the trail meets the western terminus of the Nehantic Crossover on the R (color-coded red — see Pachaug Trail). Mainline continues N, joining a gravel road at 3.3 m., which is followed to Rts. 165 and 138 at 4.5 m.

MOUNT MISERY

(U.S.G.S. quadrangles: Voluntown, Jewett City)

Starting from Rts. 165 and 138, trail wends N through woods for .2 m. to old Shetucket Turnpike and then W through woods to Rt. 49 at .5 m. Here trail turns R on highway. At 1.1 m. trail enters pine grove on L and follows wood road to junction. (Road R (unmarked) leads to ranger headquarters; road L reaches shelter near shore of Beachdale Pond.) At 1.5 m. trail crosses road and continues through woods to junction with Pachaug Trail and then to the Herman Haupt Chapman Management Area (Old Camp Lonergan) at 2 m. From here the Nehantic Trail shares the route with Pachaug Trail. It follows road out of camp and turns R into woods and through rhododendron sanctuary at 2.3 m., then joins tote road at 2.7 m. It proceeds through woods to a forest road, which it crosses at 3 m. Trail ascends to viewpoint on ledge, descends to brook and then climbs steeply to summit of Mt. Misery (441 ft.) at 3.7 m. Trail descends sharply to parking area from which it follows several woods roads to trail junction at 4.2 m. (Pachaug Trail goes L.) Nehantic Trail goes R, following roads and woods trail N to a Forest rd. at 5.2 m.

STONE HILL, HOPEVILLE POND

(U.S.G.S. quadrangle: Jewett City)

Starting at Forest rd., trail continues through blueberry patches and woods to Stone Hill and joins tote road which it follows to Breakneck Hill Rd. at 1.4 m. (The southwest terminus of the Quinebaug Trail is about 0.5 m. R (N) on this rd.)

Trail crosses road and descends through paper birches to tote road and then to Banjo Sullivan Rd. at 2.1 m. Trail crosses Banjo Sullivan Rd. and follows cartpaths to Roode Rd. at 2.7 m. Trail continues through pine grove, passing fire hole, and climbs to ridge with view. At 3.7 m. trail reaches bluff overlooking Hopeville Pond State Park, then descends to parking area at 3.9 m.

NIPMUCK TRAIL

The Nipmuck Trail runs from the town of Mansfield north to the Nipmuck State Forest in the town of Union on the Massachusetts border. The Nipmucks were an Algonquin Indian tribe that lived in what is now central Massachusetts.

See Nipmuck Trail Maps No. 1 and No. 2.

The Nipmuck Trail has two southern branches in Mansfield: one starting at Puddin' La., .8 mile W of Storrs Rd. (Rt. 195) and the other starting on the far side of the pine grove picnic area of Mansfield Hollow State Park on Bassetts Bridge Rd., .9 mile E of Storrs Rd. (Rt. 195).

PUDDIN' LANE NORTH

(U.S.G.S. quadrangles Willimantic, Spring Hill)

Puddin' La. branches W from Storrs Rd. (Rt. 195) opposite the Willimantic Reservoir, 2 m. N of the intersection of Rts. 195 and 6.

- 0.00 Starting at Puddin' La. next to large boulder proceed N through woods, cross power line continuing through woods to Wolf Rock Nature Preserve on woods rd. known as Blacksmith Rd.
- 1.95 After a short climb from Blacksmith Rd., reach Wolf Rock cliff with fine view to the S.
- 2.20 Crane Hill Rd. crossing.
- 2.45 Brown's Rd. Turn R, go a short distance, turn L and re-enter woods on N side of rd. Reach Schoolhouse Brook Park in about .25 m.
- 3.55 Clovermill Rd. crossing. Continue through park with brook and Bicentennial Pond. (Numerous side trails are available in this 500-acre park.)
- 4.45 Spring Hill Rd. Turn R on this paved rd. and follow .2 m. to Storrs Rd. (Rt. 195).
- 4.65 Turn L on Storrs Rd. a short distance to entrance of the Spring Hill Isolation Farm. Enter driveway, follow to R. Turn L at end of driveway and follow a fence (overgrown with bittersweet) along the edge of a field to a stile over a barbed wire fence. Go over stile and cross field to second stile. Climb over stile and turn R to L turn on to a gas pipeline right-of-way.
- 4.87 Turn L on right-of-way and follow it about 0.1 m. (Rapid growth of grass and brush make trail indistinct here at times.) *Look for turn.*
- 4.95 Turn R into moist woods.
- 5.25 Jct. in woods with other southern branch (from Mansfield Hollow).

MANSFIELD HOLLOW STATE PARK TO WESTFORD

(U.S.G.S. quadrangles: Spring Hill, Westford)

Parking is available year 'round in a parking lot adjacent to Bassetts Bridge Rd. at the park entrance. To reach the start of the trail follow the dirt park rd. about .25 m. across the field to the pine grove picnic area. Trail starts on another dirt rd. on the N side of the picnic area. In warm weather when the park gate is open one can drive to the picnic area and park there.

- 0.00 Leaving the dirt rd. the trail proceeds N through woods with many ups and downs and turns.
- 0.90 Trail reaches a wide woods rd. and turns R.
- 1.00 Woods rd. and trail make R angle turn.
- 1.15 Reach playing field after L turn.
- 1.25 Cross Warrenville Rd. (Rt. 89—parking here) and go L a short distance. Proceed through a mixture of fields and woods. *Watch for turns.*
- 1.75 Reach Fenton River which is crossed on a utility pole bridge (This bridge and a similar one upstream are sometimes dislodged by flooding. If so, either wade across or return to alternate white-blazed trail 500 ft. back. If bridge is missing when hiking south turn L up gravel rd. and look for R turn of cross country ski trail that leads to Warrenville Rd. (Rt. 89). Follow Rt. 89 S about .25 m. to trail crossing.)

******

ALTERNATE TRAIL (White Blazes)

- 0.00 Goes L from Nipmuck Trail 500 ft. W of Fenton River. Follows gravel rd. a short distance and then turns R downhill into woods. Trail continues over interesting and variable terrain with some fine old trees and views over the flood control area.
- 0.54 Trail reaches a broad field which it crosses bearing somewhat R. It then goes along a line of brush and trees and crosses young woods to a dirt rd. The trail turns R and

crosses another field to woods. Shortly the Fenton River comes into view and the trail proceeds N along river.

0.99 Jct. with main Nipmuck Trail just after the Nipmuck crosses the river on a utility pole bridge.

******

Main Trail Continued

1.75 After crossing the river the trail turns L immediately onto dirt rd. which leads through an interesting mixture of woods and fields. At one place it follows the ridge of an esker along the river.

2.40 L turn onto a path through young woods.

2.48 Fenton River crossing on utility pole bridge (In the event bridge is missing, either wade across or bushwack N along river to Chaffeeville Rd. in about .75 m. Regain trail on other side of rd. on bridge abutment.) Trail goes N near river for about .3 m. then bends L up hill.

3.00 Cross Chaffeeville Rd. (1.2 m. from Rt. 195—parking nearby) and continue through woods.

3.70 Reach jct. with Puddin' La. branch and continue N along base of "50-foot" cliff and ledges. Trail then goes downhill steeply. At bottom of hill turn L onto woods rd. and follow to gasline right-of-way. Turn R on to gasline right-of-way and cross a large dirt rd. to a R turn into woods.

4.75 Fenton River. Cross on bridge abutment at Chaffeeville Rd. and continue upstream on E side of river to Stone Mill Rd. Follow rd. a short distance crossing Fenton River on rd. bridge.

[The Gurleyville grist mill here is an 18th century structure that belonged to Wilbur Cross' father. It now belongs to Joshua's Trust and is open to visitors on Sundays during the tourist season.]

Shortly there is a R turn, with the trail continuing upstream.

6.50 Cross Gurleyville Rd. (parking), go R short distance and continue upstream

	through woods, across a large field and back into woods, always with the river on the R.
8.50	Turn R on dirt Old Turnpike Rd. Follow it to Rt. 44. Turn L down the hwy. about .1 m. and turn R along fence near driveway.
8.75	Follow trail along fence on R on 20 ft. wide right-of-way leading to a fine natural area along the Fenton River. Trail passes through a pine plantation before reaching the river, which it generally follows through a delightful hemlock grove, after which it bends R to leave the river.
10.00	Cross dirt Mason Rd.
10.90	Cross paved Marsh Rd. Proceed through woods approx. 2 m. to a woods rd. where the trail turns L. After about .33 m. trail turns R into the woods and downhill to a brook in a hemlock grove.
13.75	Follow Rt. 74 to the R a short distance over brook. Trail enters woods on the other side.
15.00	Cross Perry Hill Rd. Trail continues through woods.
17.00	Cross Westford Hill Rd.
17.25	Turn R on dirt Oakes Rd. and go downhill to and over Hope River. On the other side of the river the rd. becomes paved.
18.00	Turn L on Rt. 89. Trail turns R off hwy. into woods. Trail crosses field to enter State Forest on opposite side. Trail comes out on woods rd. which it follows to the R. [This rd. was originally part of the Great Trail that connected Boston and Hartford. This was the route followed by Thomas Hooker, "the Father of Connecticut."] The rd. crosses a small branch of Hope River.
18.40	Trail is joined by the Natchaug Trail on the R.
20.00	Cross Eastford-Westford Rd.

YALE FOREST

(U.S.G.S. quadrangle: Westford)

Starting at a point on N side of the Westford-Eastford Road (Chism Road) about 1 m. E of Westford Center, the trail enters Yale Forest. (*This is private land; no camping or fires.*) The trail crosses the dirt Boston Hollow Rd. at 21.6 m., then ascends a beautiful ridge on the NW side of the road and reaches viewpoints at the edge of cliffs at 22.1 m.

Shortly thereafter the trail makes a gradual 180° turn to the R to continue N through Yale Forest. The trail reaches an overlook of a tributary of Bigelow Brook at 25.0 m. and comes out on dirt Kinney Hollow (otherwise known as Axe Factory Rd.) near Bigelow Brook at 25.5 m. Trail turns R on Kinney Hollow Rd., crosses Bigelow Brook, turns L, follows along brook, and at 27.5 m. it crosses an old dirt road. It continues to Walker Mtn. (1,077 ft.), the highest point on the Nipmuck Trail at 28.3 m. Trail descends through white birch stand to Rt. 171 at 29.3 m. The entrance to Bigelow Hollow State Park (parking) is 400 ft. to the W (L) of this point.

BIGELOW HOLLOW STATE PARK AND VICINITY

(U.S.G.S. quadrangles: Eastford, Westford, Southbridge, Mass.-Conn., Wales, Mass.-Conn.)

The trails in the area N of Rt. 171 are almost exclusively on land designated as Bigelow Hollow State Park or Nipmuck State Forest; the exceptions are brief incursions into Massachusetts at the N end of Breakneck Pond and at the N end of Cat Rocks Ridge.

Within this region are three large ponds; Bigelow Pond, the smallest, is over ½ mile long. Pond view trails go completely around both Bigelow and Breakneck Ponds; there is a short section of pond view trail at the S end of Mashapaug Pond. In addition to these pond view trails, there are two upland trails: the blue blazed trail (3.9 mi.) continues the main Nipmuck Trail from its Yale Forest exit on Rt. 171 to the State Line at the E shore of Breakneck Pond; the blue blazed— white bar Ridge Trail (4.3 mi.) begins on the paved Park road near the N end of Bigelow Pond and also ends at Breakneck Pond at the State Line, on the W shore.

Both the yellow blazed trails are short and without steep hills. From Mashapaug Pond boat launch (at end of paved road) to the S shore of the Pond and return is about 1 mile; from any of the parking areas off the paved Park road a walk around Bigelow Pond is about 2 miles. Another easy, but much longer hike, is the walk from N end of Bigelow Pond, along the unpaved road to Breakneck Pond, then along the E shore trail. This road walk is 2½ mi. round trip; the E shore trail is 2½ mi. to the N end of Breakneck Pond, but one could walk part way, then return. However, a minimum Breakneck Pond view walk should include at least 4 mi. from the Park to the N end of Breakneck Pond is 7½ mi. round trip.

Experienced hikers can undertake various loop hikes which may include parts or all of the Breakneck Pond View Trail, part of the main Nipmuck Trail, and/or the white bar Ridge Trail. These hikes include some stretches of steep climbs, difficult footing, and distances of 8 to 10 miles round trip. For these more difficult trails, hiking shoes are recommended.

White blazes are used in a few areas to indicate connectors to the blue blazed trails. All the trails in this area permit loop hikes from the paved Park road. The unpaved roads leading N from the N end of Breakneck Pond lead into a swamp or other unimproved roads in Southbridge, Mass.

Within the Park there are several designated parking areas; most are W of the paved road; one is E (about 0.3 mi. from Rt. 171) and provides white blazed trail access to the thru Nipmuck Trail. Hikers should avoid parking at the fisherman's parking area near Rt. 171 and at the boat launch at Mashapaug Pond.

In the following detailed trail descriptions the only streams noted are those that may be difficult for dry shoe crossings in Spring, during rainy periods, and after heavy rains. The most steep trail area is on the E slope of Cat Rocks ridge—the white bar Ridge trail. There are several caves on the E slope of the Cat Rocks ridge; but there are no developed trails to the caves and footing is difficult/hazardous.

Each of the following trails is notated from the Bigelow Park area or from S to N.

Nipmuck Thru Trail

Blue Blazes

0.0 Begin on Rt. 171 opposite trail exit from Yale Forest. Short distance: left turn off unpaved road.

0.2	Jct. white blazed trail (L) to parking area and paved State Park road.
0.3	Stone wall pass thru; house foundation.
0.4	Stream crossing; unpaved road crossing; swamp crossing.
0.5	Pile of large, flat rocks.
1.8	Unpaved road crossing: L 0.1 mi (L at first fork) to jct. Breakneck Pond View Trails. At jct.: R to east shore trail, straight to West Pond View Trail, straight on road to Mass. Road at L: 1.1 mi. to paved Park road at N end Bigelow Pond; R at first fork to E shore Breakneck Pond and Southbridge, Mass.
3.2	Unpaved road. crossing. R 0.5 mi to Carrion Rd., unpaved area, 1.0 mi to paved area. From trail jct. L 0.1 to jct. unpaved E shore road.
3.9	Thru Trail ends at Breakneck Pond shore and State Line marker; also jct. with E Pond View Trail.
4.3	R on shore road, then L around N end of Pond to jct. Ridge Trail (R 4.3 mi to paved Park road near N end Bigelow Pond.). Also jct W. Pond View Trail.

CONNECTOR ROAD (UNPAVED)

White Blazes

N End Bigelow Pond Parking/Picnic Area to Breakneck Pond (Northbound)

0.0	Parking/Picnic Area
0.1	Quarry area
0.3	Rd. jct.: L to Breakneck Pond
1.1	End of Connector Road: L fork to Breakneck Pond trails; R fork 0.1 m. to crossing of thru Nipmuck Trail

Breakneck Pond View Trails

Blue-blazed with center white dot.

These trails generally follow the edge of Breakneck Pond with many pond edge clearings suitable for picnics. Unpaved rd. from pavement in park at end of Bigelow Pond to Pond View trails is 1.1 m.

EAST BREAKNECK POND VIEW TRAIL

White Dot—Blue Blazes

0.0	Unpaved rd. SE to Nipmuck Trail, NW to

	West Pond View Trail. SW on unpaved rd. 1.1 m. to Bigelow Pond.
0.1	Trail turns R to pond side lookout.
0.2	Unpaved rd. to shore edge.
0.3	Stream crossing.
0.4	Picnic area.
0.5	Stream crossing, then picnic area, with rd. entry.
0.7	Picnic area rd. entry.
0.8	Stream crossing.
1.0	Stream crossing.
1.1	Stream crossing.
1.5	Lookout to pond.
1.7	Stream crossing, rd. entry.
1.8	Unpaved rd. jct.; trail on rd.
1.9	End of trail; State Line marker; Nipmuck Trail to R 0.25 m. around Pond end to Ridge Trail and West Pond View Trail.

West Breakneck Pond View Trail

White Dot—Blue Blazes

Each noted hilltop requires additional climb of 100-200 ft.

0.0	Trail starts at jct. with E Pond View Trail and unpaved Connector Road from Bigelow Pond (1.1 m.).
0.2	Far end of peninsula: pond view.
0.3	Road jct, turn R; road often flooded. Trail R off road.
0.4	Start shore rock area; difficult footing.
0.5	End rock area.
0.7	Hilltop.
0.9	Drive-in picnic area.
1.2	Water crossing, beaver dam; beaver lodge.
1.4	Island access, pond views. (Easy dry season crossing.)
1.7	Lookout rock; hilltop.
1.8	Hilltop.
2.0	Hilltop.
2.1	Side trail (R) to lookout.
2.2	Road jct, Ridge Trail jct., State Line, stream crossing. R .3 m. to jct. E. Pond View and Nipmuck Thru Trails.

Ridge Trail

White Bar-Blue Blazes

From main rd. in Bigelow Hollow Park; trail starts about 0.1 m. from parking area, N end of

Bigelow Pond and 0.3 m. S from Mashapaug Pond boat landing.

- 0.0 Pavement at trail entry; also white-blazed trail.
- 0.1 White-blazed trail turn off to hill top.
- 0.2 Stream crossing, then white-blazed trail jct. (White-blazed trail to N-bound unpaved rd.) Ridge Trail makes U-turn. 720' elev.
- 0.3 High point at S end of ridge.
- 1.2 Look-out to Breakneck Pond; pond not visible during foilage season.
- 1.5 Unpaved rd. crossing.
- 1.8 W peak.
- 2.0 E peak 1020' elev.
- 2.5 Unpaved rd. jct.
- 2.6 Turn off rd.
- 2.8 Stream crossing. 750' elev.
- 3.0 Turn off to caves.
- 3.1 S lookout. 920' elev.
- 3.3 N lookout. Begin steep descent.
- 3.5 Boulders.
- 3.6 Stream crossing. 720' elev.
- 4.3 Trail end; unpaved rd. Jct. West Pond View Trail. State line. L around pond end ¼ m. to Nipmuck and East Pond View Trails. Major stream crossing at W shore entry into Mass.

BIGELOW POND LOOP TRAIL

Yellow Blazes

Bigelow Pond Trail circuits the entire Pond. Highlights of the walk are the picnic area at the N end of the Pond and on the island along the E shore. Travel clockwise:

- 0.0 Pond shore parking area about 0.4 m. from Rt. 171.
- 0.1 Rd. to island.
- 0.4 Dam, Rt. 171 jct.
- 0.5 Far side of pond, trail turn.
- 0.7 Island viewpoint.
- 1.1 Bridge over stream at pond end; trail turn.
- 1.2 Rd. side parking, picnic area.
- 1.4 Stream crossing.
- 1.6 Pond circuit completed.

MASHAPAUG TRAIL

Yellow Blazes

This trail at the S end of the pond provides a walk-way from the boat launch area parking to a small rocky island with excellent views of the pond. To date this trail has not yet been blazed as a loop, but the foot paths along the pond shore are very evident.

- 0.0 Pavement at boat launch; picnic area rd. pipe gate.
- 0.1 Turn off to trail. If no turn, 0.1 m. to pond and picnic area.
- 0.4 Pond edge, trail turns R to viewpoint.
- 0.6 Viewpoint; picnic area.
- 1.0 Return to pavement along pond edge trail—not blazed.

OLD FURNACE TRAIL

(U.S.G.S. quadrangle: East Killingly)

The trail starts on the W side of the park entrance, which is on the S side of Rt. 6 about ½ mile E of Exit 91 of I-395. It proceeds S along a path through a hemlock grove to a marshy pond, crosses dam, enters marshy pond on R and goes for about a mile to summit of high ledges overlooking Half Hill Pond. It continues for another mile to emerge on Squaw Rock Rd., which it follows S to the ramp entering the Rt. 6 Connector. It parallels the ramp in the woods on state highway property and then turns S. The trail ends about a mile away at Squaw Rock. Total mileage 4.0 m.

See map Old Furnace Trail.

PACHAUG TRAIL

The Pachaug Trail is primarily a woodland trail in the wild, rugged region of southeastern Connecticut and southwestern Rhode Island, extending for about 30 miles, from Green Fall Pond to Pachaug Pond. It passes beautiful ponds, pretty streams, and striking rock formations. It proceeds through stands of conifers and hardwoods and a rhododendron sanctuary. It is entirely within state land. See maps, Nehantic Trail, Pachaug Trail, and Quinebaug Trail, Pachaug Trail.

GREEN FALL POND

(U.S.G.S. quadrangle: Voluntown)

Pachaug Trail (blazed blue) starts at the Green Fall Pond picnic area (camping and other recreational facilities) on the Green Fall Rd. Near this location the Nehantic Trail (blazed blue) and the *Narragansett Crossover* converge.

[The *Narragansett Crossover* (color-coded red) goes E 0.2 m. through laurel to connect with the Narragansett Trail near the R. I. border.]

Pachaug Trail follows Green Fall Road for .14 m. and, across from the *Narragansett Crossover* turns L and continues over rock outcrops and a brook to the junction with a loop trail (color-coded yellow) at the base of Rabbit Ledge (loop traverses a gully at the base of the ledge for .11 m.).

The mainline climbs a moderately steep slope on the L to the summit of a ledge and goes on to meet the N terminus of the loop; it crosses a motorcycle trail at .86 m. and continues N on a wood road. At 1.05 m. the main route departs from the wood road on the R. (Wood road goes to Tarklin Hill Rd.) This is the junction with the eastern terminus of the *Nehantic Crossover*.

[The *Nehantic Crossover* (color-coded red) goes W 1.5 m. to the Nehantic Trail, ascending and descending the slopes of a 500-ft. hill, through dense thickets of laurel.]

The main trail proceeds over fairly level terrain and, approaching a watershed, passes over a series of moderately steep ascents and descents; it passes through a rocky glen at 1.69 m. and crosses Green Fall River (brook) in a deep gully near its source at 1.76 m. Trail then rambles over rock outcroppings and passes an access (color-coded yellow) path that leads to Green Fall Rd.; trail descends a watershed on the E slope and crosses Rt. 138 at 2.4 m. Trail proceeds N and immediately meets the southern terminus of a loop (color-coded yellow) on the R. The mainline pursues its course on the L to meet the N terminus of the loop at 2.9 m. After crossing a wood road and a brook, the trail progresses through a white pine forest to come to the Tippecansett Crossover on the R.

[The *Tippecansett Crossover* (color-coded red) goes E 0.5 m. through plantations of red pine to the Tippecansett Trail in R. I.]

Pachaug Trail goes L on the cartpath and then swings R on another cartpath; it goes several yds. over a boggy area, crosses a brook, then along the red-pine-clad crest of an esker sandwiched between two spruce bogs. It meanders over more red pine plantations to emerge eventually on Rt. 165 at 3.78 m. Trail turns R, following the highway and the shore of Beach Pond, to the Conn.-R. I. State Line at 4.11 m. Trail continues to the beach area of the park at 4.4 m.

BEACH POND

(U.S.G.S. quadrangle: Voluntown)

From the beach area the Pachaug Trail shares the route with the yellow-blazed Tippecansett Trail (Rhode Island) (see *A. M. C. Mass–R.I. Trail Guide*). Trail ascends and continues along a high, fairly steep bluff on the E shore of the pond (excellent views) and then skirts the end of picnic area on the crest of a steep slope.

At .5 m. the trail departs from the Tippecansett Trail on the L, proceeds NW over a pine-crested esker to emerge again on the shore of the pond. It follows the shore briefly, and then plunges into a large hemlock grove. It crosses a brook and then ascends a gentle slope to a crest. The trail descends to another pine-crested esker and follows this to the shore of the pond (excellent views).

Trail departs from the pond again, parallels a stream, and then winds to a crossover trail at 1.5 m. connecting with the Tippecansett Trail (.3 m. uphill). Trail crosses stream before entering a series of pine groves, where it crosses the R.I.—Conn. State Line to enter Voluntown, Conn. Marked trees indicate approx. location of State Line at 1.75 m.

The trail continues W and then S along the base of an 80-ft. precipice. It swings sharply W again (R), climbing a rocky defile between ledges, and then over and around more rocks and precipices. At a point the trail passes a few feet from an old Indian shelter. The trail reaches the Connecticut boat launch site on the N shore of Beach Pond at 3.16 m. (limited sanitary facilities) — splendid views of Beach Pond.

From the parking area the trail takes a northerly direction and after crossing a wood road, descends steeply into a short, narrow, deep gorge, comes out into the open, turns R and ascends briefly, then continues along the base of a series of cliffs that rise abruptly to about 60 ft. Large hemlocks and pine abound.

The trail splits into two routes: one is an easy course along the base; the other climbs to and goes through the "lemon squeezer," a narrow passage between the cliff and a large slab of rock. The routes merge at the crossing of a brook.

Trail crosses a forest road and continues to another forest road at 4.94 m. (White-blazed Canonicus Trail goes R. *(See below.)* Trail then proceeds along a cartpath on L and crosses Shetucket Turnpike at 5.26 m.

Canonicus Trail

This white-blazed trail starts on a forest road at its junction with the Pachaug Trail .32 m. S of Shetucket Tpke. It goes 2.5 m. E, N and E again to the Escoheag Hill Lookout Tower in R.I., where it forms a junction with the Tippecansett Trail. (1 m. E on the Tippencansett are the beautiful Stepstone Falls and the Ben Utter Trail.) (See *Mass & R.I. Trail Guide, A.M.C.*) See map Nehantic Trail, Pachaug Trail.

DAWLEY POND AND EKONK HILL

(U.S.G.S. quadrangle: Voluntown)

Trail passes through wildlife area and crosses a causeway of a wildlife pond, follows a cartpath, crosses a forest road near the site of an abandoned farm, and continues on a cartpath to a junction; turns L and proceeds E of Dawley Pond. Trail crosses brook at .85 m. and continues on a path through spruce and pine areas to a forest road at 1.33 m. Trail crosses road at site of another abandoned farm and proceeds through more wildlife areas, crosses a brook and an abandoned dike. (On L an unmarked trail leads to an old family cemetery.)

At 1.89 m. the trail emerges on the shore of Great Meadow Pond. Trail crosses a long causeway to a wood road, follows it briefly to a junction. The trail turns R, follows a cartpath near the shore of the pond, passes through groves of larch and pine, and at 2.63 m. crosses the causeway of another pond. Trail emerges on a forest road at 3.06 m., follows it briefly, and follows a tote road on the L for a short distance. Trail leaves tote road, turns R and proceeds to forest road which it parallels for a considerable distance.

Trail wanders from forest road occasionally, but always returns. At 4.1 m. it crosses the road and enters the town of Sterling. (The road, white-blazed, provides an easy alternative route.) The scenic trail route proceeds to the Porter Pond picnic area and crosses Wood River on a foot bridge at 4.32 m.

The trail crosses Brown Rd. at Porter Pond picnic area and continues to the dam at Porter Pond, crossing Wood River below the dam. The trail climbs to the site of an abandoned farm and then follows a tote road, crossing a stream, the outlet of Cedar Swamp. The trail turns L from the tote road on to Cedar Swamp Rd. The white-blazed Pharisee Rock Trail starts here on the tote road. *(See below.)* The main trail skirts Cedar Swamp and proceeds through the woods, reaching the site of the Corey Homestead at 1.85 m. (sanitary facilities).

Pharisee Rock Trail

The trail, blazed white, starts at the junction of a tote road and the Cedar Swamp Rd., directly across from the blue-blazed Pachaug Trail, and proceeds E. At .2 m. it swings sharply L with the cartpath and goes N. At .6 m. it crosses an outflow of a wildlife marsh on the L; on the R is the site of an old sap mill. At .7 m. the trail leaves the cartpath and climbs a moderate gradient to the summit of Pharisee Rock at 1 m. (Excellent views of the crest of Ekonk Hill). See map Pachaug Trail.

HELL HOLLOW AND PHILLIPS POND

(U.S.G.S. quadrangles: Oneca, Voluntown)

The trail follows Cedar Swamp Rd. to Rt. 49 in Ekonk at 2.05 m. The trail continues W on Hell Hollow Rd. (directly across Rt. 49 from Cedar Swamp Rd.) and enters the woods on the R at 2.6

m. near the intersection of the Plainfield, Voluntown, and Sterling town lines. From there the trail follows the State Forest boundary and descends into Hell Hollow. Near the bottom of the Hollow the trail turns sharply L (S) and passes through a stand of evergreens before reaching Hell Hollow Rd. at 3.5 m.

From Hell Hollow Rd., the trail proceeds on a wood road S, passing near a spring, and continues to a junction of wood roads at 4.35 m. (A white-blazed side trail follows a wood road R .75 m. to Phillips Pond picnic area. The same trail rejoins the main trail in an additional .65 m.) The main trail continues straight and is rejoined by the Phillips Pond side trail at 4.65 m. An abandoned homestead is found nearby.

Continuing along tote roads, the trail crosses Gardiner Rd. at 5.3 m. and follows a path through a spruce grove, crossing Lowden Brook at 5.45 m. The trail climbs to higher ground, traverses an area of beech trees, returns to the brook, passing a series of cascades, and continues along the brook to the Lowden Brook picnic area at 6.7 m. (sanitary facilities).

MOUNT MISERY

(U.S.G.S. quadrangles: Voluntown, Jewett City)

The trail leaves the Lowden Brook picnic area, turns L, proceeds on a forest road about a dozen yds. to the junction with another forest road and turns L again. It follows this forest road a short distance, then turns R, onto the tote road, follows it briefly and turns R, descends a gradual slope, rises slightly, turns R, and enters hemlock forest. Trail traverses the forest to a brook, crosses, climbs to cartpath on R, follows cartpath several yds., turns L into a conifer forest and traverses it for about 1 m. to the junction with the Nehantic Trail at 1.35 m. Here the Pachaug and Nehantic Trails coincide and follow the same route for nearly 2 m. (See Nehantic Trail)

The trail continues to the Herman Haupt Chapman Management Area. (Camping, picnic, water, sanitary facilities.) Trail follows forest road, crosses Mt. Misery Brook, turns R and follows the Rhododendron Sanctuary Trail through the sanctuary to Mt. Misery Brook. Rhododendron and fair-sized white cedar abound in this swamp. (Rhododendron bloom in mid-July). This trail is passable only during late spring, summer, and autumn months.

The trail follows the return loop of the sanctuary path and turns R to traverse an area of young white cedars. It continues to a tote road, turns L to follow the tote road briefly. It turns R and continues to the forest road, crosses and proceeds through a pine grove. The trail ascends sharply to a viewpoint (excellent views), and makes a gradual descent to a brook, crosses, continues over level terrain, and abruptly ascends to the summit of Mt. Misery (El. 441 ft.) at 2.81 m. (excellent views).

Trail descends steeply on the opposite side to a parking area and follows a forest access road, crosses the road at the bend and turns L and continues to a wood road, turns R, follows the wood road to a trail junction at 3.35 m. (Nehantic Trail diverges R. See Nehantic Trail).

Pachaug Trail turns L and follows wood road along the base of an abandoned causeway of a dry pond, crosses a transmission line right-of-way at 3.45 m. Trail turns R on transmission line tote road for a short distance and turns L. After ascending to the top of a knoll to a bench mark, it proceeds through the woods to Rt. 138 at 4.74 m. [Trail is now in town of Griswold.]

PACHAUG POND

(U.S.G.S. quadrangle: Jewett City)

The trail crosses Rt. 138, turns R, and proceeds to the intersection with Rt. 201, turns L on Rt. 201 and follows it to the top of the hill at .1 m. Trail turns R (W) onto state property. The trail continues downgrade and enters woods. It crosses and recrosses brook in a low area and then ascends through a brushy field. It enters woods again, crosses a brook and proceeds to a clearing on the shore of a cove on the N shore of Pachaug Pond.

The trail traverses a level area that abounds with moccasin orchid, cuts through pine grove and re-enters a hardwood tract to emerge on the shore of Pachaug Pond (fine views), and continues to the boundary of State property at 1.45 m. The trail proceeds on Shore Drive and then zigzags along a series of short roads to Rt. 138 at

1.95 m. It follows Rt. 138 and turns L on state land going along the boundary line and a dirt road to the Pachaug Pond dam at 2.63 m. Trail returns to a tote road that follows the Pachaug River to reach Rt. 138 at 2.92 m.

PAUGUSSETT TRAIL

This trail, named for the Indians who had their chief seat at what is now Derby, begins at Indian Well State Park, runs along the Housatonic River, and ends at East Village in Monroe.

See map Kettletown State Park, Zoar Trail, Paugussett Trail.

INDIAN WELL

(U.S.G.S. quadrangles: Long Hill, Southbury)

From Rt. 110 enter Indian Well State Park, 2.5 m. N of center of Shelton.

- 0.00 Within Park cross stonewall bridge, ascend trail steeply into hemlock grove.
- 0.20 Continue on steep trail, with rocky footing, to the ridge with some views to the E.
- 0.30 One-mile loop side trail (blue blazes with yellow dots) through property of Shelton Land Trust.
- 0.40 White-blazed trail leads 0.20 m. to Park Road.
- 0.90 Cross 2 brooks to a hemlock forest.
- 1.10 Cross stream via a wooden bridge.
- 1.40 Gradually ascend to another hemlock grove.
- 1.50 Cross a couple of small brooks.
- 1.60 Continue on through a laurel grove.
- 1.70 Pass through a rockfall followed by the Hydraulic pipeline.
- 1.80 Pass by a cave.
- 1.90 Cross a brook.
- 2.00 Another brook.
- 2.10 Seasonal rocky outlook to the S.
- 2.30 Jct. with *feeder trail* that descends .80 m. to the Park Rd.
- 2.40 Continue northerly, then R, somewhat northeasterly to cross a running brook.
- 2.50 *Development anticipated; watch for relocations.*
- 2.85 Pass through Hydraulic Company property to come out on Little Fox Run Rd.

3.80 Turn R on Okenuck Way, L on Boulder Path, cross Princess Winona Way, ascend open space right-of-way (elevation 450' at the ridge). Walk across open space to cross a drainage gorge.
3.85 Thoreau Dr.: turn R to enter the woods again.
3.90 *Development in process, 1990; watch for signs and blazes.*
4.10 Cross another running brook onto cart-path bordering Webb Mtn. Park in Monroe.
4.40 Cross Park's orange trail.
4.50 Pass by Park's yellow trail.
4.55 Cross yellow trail again.
4.70 Cross red trail.
4.75 Cross over a brook.
4.80 Walk a short distance on dirt rd. in Park, then go L with a steep ascent.
5.10 Follow a rocky gorge.
5.40 Cross a brook.
5.55 Enjoy the view of the river at the LOOKOUT before descending with views of Stevenson, Lake Zoar; elevation 520'.
5.65 At the power line turn L.
5.75 Turn R onto private property, gradually descending.
5.85 Make an S turn, L, then R.
5.90 Follow old logging rd., turn L, cross stream. [Hike may be shortened at this point. Instead of turning L off the logging rd., proceed easterly over the RR tracks on the blue blazed-yellow dot trail to Rt. 34. (6.10 m.)]
5.95 After crossing stream, walk parallel with RR tracks to reach a small parking lot off Cottage St., turn R on Cottage St., passing culvert.
6.05 Turn L onto old forest rd.
6.95 Ascend slowly to Silver Mine filled with boulders.
7.10 Reach a metal gate, continuing on private property.
7.35 Come to the end of a pasture fence.
7.55 Cross Boy's Half Way River in Monroe on Hydraulic Company land.
7.65 Cross Barn Hill Rd.
7.95 Pass through Sanctuary to East Village Rd. East Village Center is .2 m. E of Rt. 111 in Monroe.

PEQUOT TRAIL

The Pequot Trail provides a link between Norwich and Lantern Hill where the hiker can continue on the Narragansett Trail to other trails in Pachaug Forest or Rhode Island. Its 10 miles become progressively more hilly and wild as the hiker approaches Lantern Hill with fine views at Rose Hill and just E of Shewville Rd. See map Pequot Trail, Narragansett Trail.

HELL GATE

(U.S.G.S. quadrangles: Norwich, Uncasville)

The trail commences about 1 m. E of Norwich on Rt. 165 near the power line, opposite Old Jewett City Rd. (parking). Trail proceeds S and turning L from power line enters woods. Returning to power line it goes W to top of ledge, descends to brook crossing and continues along power line. Then it turns L and under power line to E side, crosses fenced land (hikers only) to view at 1.3 m. Trail descends to L turn onto wood rd., continues to W side of power line, descending to brook in ravine. At 2 m. trail crosses to E side of power line and through pasture to gateway at 2.5 m. Trail turns R and continues S to Rt. 2 at 3.5 m.

ROSE HILL

(U.S.G.S. quadrangles: Uncasville, Old Mystic)

From Rt. 2 trail follows Lincoln Park Rd. to brick building at .6 m. Turn L around ballfield, through evergreens on a slope, crossing Rose Hill Rd. and passing L of house onto state land. Trail enters woods and leads to Rose Hill (*aka* Thomas Mt.) with extensive view. After following the rim, trail turns L around pasture, through woods, past sand quarry on L onto Thomas Rd., which it follows L. At 2.6 m. it turns R on Mathewson Mill Rd., then L on Fanning Rd. and R into woods. Trail leaves woods between two houses onto Coachman Pike. Turn L to Shewville Rd.

MUSHANTUXET

(U.S.G.S. quadrangle: Old Mystic)

Turning R, trail follows Shewville Rd. .4 m. then turns L into woods and slabs hill to excellent lookout at .5 m. to S and W. Stay on trail in this Western Pequot Indian land area. After a rough, rocky area, trail follows S edge of cedar swamp to brook, through rhododendrons to old rd. at 2.4 m. Trail turns L on this rd. to Rt. 214, Indiantown Rd., then L for .1 m. to Lantern Hill Rd., and R on this rd. for .1 m. Here trail turns into woods on L and after about .4 m. joins the Narragansett Trail in saddle to N of Lantern Hill at 3.4 m. (Rt. 2 is .4 m. L along Narragansett Trail; summit of Lantern Hill .3 m. R on same trail.)

PINE KNOB LOOP TRAIL

(U.S.G.S. quadrangle: Ellsworth)

This 2.5 mile trail is located in Housatonic Meadows State Park and Housatonic State Forest on the W side of the Housatonic River N of Cornwall Bridge. It climbs 700 feet to beautiful vistas over the river valley. There is direct access to the trail from the state park's camp grounds and group camp area. See map Pine Knob Loop Trail.

Trail starts from parking area on the W side of U.S. 7, (1.1 m. N of Cornwall Bridge), crosses Hatch Brook and proceeds N through pine woods. (Red-blazed trail goes L and ascends NW near Hatch Brook in hemlock-clad ravine with picturesque cascades, finally rejoining main trail.) At .2 m. beginning of loop is reached. Continue north, crossing small brooks. At .4 m. turn L. (Trail R leads to meadow bordering U.S. 7, with campground across highway.) In 75 yds. trail reaches another jct. (Side trail R leads to group camp area, with spur to N end of meadow across hwy. from campground.)

Trail ascends sharply, reaching scenic section at .7 m., descends slightly into saddle, and climbs steeply up Pine Knob. It reaches top of cliffs at .9 m. with splendid broad view S over Housatonic Valley and surrounding highlands. Trail turns NW over wooded summit of Pine Knob (1,120 ft.), with narrow view N up Housatonic Valley, drops to saddle at 1.1 m., and ascends to view of Pine Knob at 1.2 m., (At this point the Appalachian Trail joins the Pine Knob Loop Trail for about ¾ m.) The trail continues S along crest. At end of crest (1.5 m.) there is beautiful view SE over river valley to Cornwall Bridge. Trail descends SW to junction at 1.8 m., turns L and descends SE, paralleling Hatch Brook. (Previously mentioned red-blazed trail comes in on R. From this point the A.T. continues S, after crossing Hatch Brook.) Trail reaches starting point of loop at 2.3 m. Turn R to return to parking area at 2.5 m.

QUINEBAUG TRAIL

(U.S.G.S. quadrangles: Oneco, Plainfield, Voluntown, Jewett City)

See map Quinebaug Trail.

The trail begins on Spaulding Rd. in Plainfield (.4 m. S of Rt. 14A). It goes E along a sunken cartpath for about .1 m. to Lockes Meadow Pond and then along its W bank for .4 m. to Downing Rd. It follows this road for .2 m. to its intersection with Flat Rock Rd. (Quinebaug Crossover, color-coded yellow, goes L to the Pachaug Trail).

The main trail bears R on Flat Rock Rd., descending to a sag. (A short trail leads L to Devil:s Den). The Quinebaug ascends the solid rock watershed road to the summit (views). Trail turns L on a cartpath and follows this for 1.2 m. to Hell Hollow Rd. (On the L, road leads to Hell Hollow Pond and Pachaug Trail.) Main trail crosses road on the R and continues on the cartpath .8 m. to the picnic area at S end of Phillips Pond. [The picnic area can be reached by unpaved Trail Rd. (a forest rd.) that runs S from Hell Hollow Rd. about 0.5 m. E of Breakneck Hill Rd.]

The trail crosses road and also a rifle range — *on the safe side* — and continues on a wood road for 1 m. to Breakneck Hill Rd. Entire route: 5.5 m. Continuing S. on this rd. about 0.5 m. leads to crossing of Nehantic Trail.

[In earlier editions of *The Walk Book* the portion of the Quinebaug Trail from Phillips Pond to Breakneck Hill Rd. was called "Castle Trail", because of the ruins of a "castle" W of Breakneck Hill Rd.]

QUINNIPIAC TRAIL

The Quinnipiac Trail, the oldest in the Connecticut Blue Trail System, was started by Edgar L. Heermance in 1928. It follows a series of trap rock ridges. Although essentially a wooded trail, it passes over the Sleeping Giant and Mt. Sanford with excellent views. Total length of the trail from North Haven to Cheshire is about 21 miles. See map Trails North of New Haven.

NORTH HAVEN-QUINNIPIAC RIVER STATE PARK

(U.S.G.S. quadrangle: Wallingford)

The trail starts at a point .1 m. S of the end of Banton St. in North Haven. Banton St. begins on the E (R) side of State St. about .3 m. N of the intersection of Rts. 5 and 22, just before State St. crosses the Wilbur Cross Pkwy.

The trail passes 2 m. through woods of the town of North Haven and enters Quinnipiac River State Park. The trail continues through woods and overgrown fields on the W bank of the Quinnipiac River for about 3.2 m. and reaches Toelles Rd. at 3.4 m. The trail turns W (L) on Toelles Rd., passes under the Wilbur Cross Parkway, and turns S (L) on the Old Hartford Turnpike for about .1 m. to enter Sleeping Giant State Park at 3.6 m.

This section of trail is not passable during periods of high water on the Quinnipiac River.

SLEEPING GIANT

(U.S.G.S. quadrangles: Wallingford, Mount Carmel)

The Quinnipiac Trail enters Sleeping Giant State Park from Old Hartford Tpke. about 100 yds. S of the Wallingford-North Haven town line. The trail passes over the *right foot* of the Giant to Hezekiah's Knob at 1.9 m. From there it passes over the *left knee* and *left thigh* of the Giant to the Stone Tower at 3.5 m.

Continuing W, the trail crosses the *waist*, the N side of the *chest* and *neck* to the *chin* with broad panoramic views of Long Island Sound. It then passes over the *head*, descends steeply along the S side of a quarry and over the *elbow* to the Mill

River bridge at 5.1 m. It continues out of the Park and along Mt. Carmel Ave. to Whitney Ave. (Rt. 10) at 5.2 m.

[There is a network of about 30 m. of trails in Sleeping Giant State Park. The principal ones are described in a separate chapter—see p. 88.]

YORK MOUNTAIN AND MAD MARE'S HILL

(U.S.G.S. quadrangle: Mount Carmel)

The trail follows West Woods Rd. W from Whitney Ave., just N of the entrance to Sleeping Giant Park. After .2 m the trail turns L on Kimberly Rd. After crossing W ridge of York Hill with good views up the Cheshire vale, trail runs S (views to East Rock) to attractive hemlock ridge and continues via Rocky Top Rd. to Shepard Ave. at 1.2 m. It follows the road L past Hamden Public Works garage to R turn on Nolan Rd. It turns R again at T and L to brook in channel of green moss at 1.8 m.

The trail reaches summit of York Mtn. (el. 680 ft.) at 2.4 m. It goes along S and W sides with succession of good views from cliffs. (At SW corner, side trail descends sharply to Sanford Notch and connection with Regicides Trail.)

Quinnipiac Trail continues down to Bethany Gap at Gaylord Mtn. Rd. at 4 m. Here trail turns W 150 ft. N of dam, climbs steep Mad Mare's Hill with good views to E and W, and follows W ridge. It passes abandoned cottage at 4.5 m., crosses power line and climbs to picturesque hemlock ridge, at 5.5 m. From the ridge it goes down gradual slope and recrosses Gaylord Mtn. Rd. near West Woods cemetery at 6.6 m.

MOUNT SANFORD AND ROARING BROOK

(U.S.G.S. quadrangles: Mount Carmel, Southington)

The trail follows Downes Rd. N to sign for YMCA Camp Laurel at .5 m. At this point a feeder trail (blue/red dot blazes) enters R. (This feeder trail forms a 2.3 m. loop, which emerges on another feeder trail, described later in this section, .1 m. S of George A Cromie Memorial Grove.) Main trail goes through gate and at .2 m.

it turns L. (Feeder trail (blue/red dot blazes) to Cromie Memorial Grove with conifer plantings and three shelters continues on wood road. At .7 m. it turns L into woods and rejoins main trail in Nettleton's Ravine at 1.4 m.)

Main trail follows wood road past swimming pools and camp buildings. At .9 m. trail turns R into woods and climbs short, steep grade to Mt. Sanford (el. 820 ft.) — good view W into Prospect. It continues to Nettleton's Ravine and Bethany Mtn. Rd. (Rt. 42) at 2.5 m.

Trail bears R on highway, enters woods and ascends hill, passes several ridges with occasional lookouts and reaches Roaring Brook Falls at 3.9 m. (Feeder trail bears L to Roaring Brook Rd., Prospect, at .5 m.)

Main trail crosses brook and continues over ridges to old road at 5.8 m. (A continuation of Cornwall Ave., but impassable for cars.) It turns L and at crossroads, turns R on Tress Rd. and turns L on Chatfield Rd. to Rt. 68 at 6.7 m.

RAGGED MOUNTAIN PRESERVE TRAIL

(U.S.G.S. quadrangles: Meriden, New Britain)

This 6 mile loop trail is in Berlin's Ragged Mountain Preserve and on New Britain Water Co. property. It goes along attractive ledges overlooking the Hart Ponds, joins the Metacomet Trail on Ragged Mountain for about 1.5 m. and circles back to its starting point. Blazes are blue with a red dot. See map Metacomet Trail, Rt. 15 to U.S. 6.

The main access to the loop is at the entrance to Ragged Mountain Preserve .6 m. W of the Chamberlain Highway (Rt. 71A) on West Lane. In about 300 ft. the trail splits. Going L, paths and old woods roads lead to the ledges overlooking the Hart Ponds in .6 m. At 1.2 m. is a cliff with a free standing wall that appears almost manmade. The trail continues along the ledges for another .5 m. with many good outlooks to the Ponds below as well as to the Hanging Hills of Meriden until the Metacomet Trail is reached at the top of Ragged Mt. at 1.7 m. The loop now follows the Metacomet (blue blazes) N until at 3.1

m. it turns R (E). Now the blazes with red dots follow mostly old wood roads until at 4.1 m. the trail turns R to go over and along several low ridges, beside a brook, and then at 4.4 m. to a junction with the feeder trail from Shuttlemeadow Ave. (See below.) At 5.1 m. the trail leaves a wood road to turn sharply R along a small stream (often dry in summer but very attractive in spring). At the top of the falls is some interesting stone work. Now the loop continues along the ridge for a little over a half mile, descends, turns sharply R on a woods road at 5.8 m. and returns to the entrance of the Preserve at 6 m.

The alternate entrance to the loop is on Shuttlemeadow Ave. 1.1 m. W of Corbin Ave. This is just a few feet E of the point where the Metacomet Trail leaves Shuttlemeadow Ave. headed N. The feeder trail, also blazed blue with red dots, goes E along an old water supply canal for .6 m. to join the main loop.

REGICIDES TRAIL

The Regicides Trail follows the crest of the West Rock range, NW of New Haven, to Sanford Notch (Lower Bethany Gap), where connection is made with the Quinnipiac Trail. It was named for the regicides Whalley and Goffe who found refuge in Judges' Cave. It is one of Connecticut's most spectacular cliff walks; the 6 miles of trail have no assured water supply and, in places, difficult footing. See map Trails North of New Haven.

SOUTHERN RANGE

(U.S.G.S. quadrangles: New Haven, Mount Carmel)

Regicides Trail starts at Judges' Cave (accessible by car or by feeder trail beginning at back of baseball park near foot of West Rock. Trail ascends West Rock and reaches cave in 1.3 m. Alternate entrance to feeder at Springside Ave., .5 m. from junction with Blake St.) and continues N, at first on old paths, along W scarp of West Rock ridge. In .5 m cross bridle path while descending to Buttress Gap. (Unmarked path E to Baldwin Parkway entrance, Wintergreen Falls and Springside Ave., .2 m.) From Buttress Gap ascend steep slope to top of ridge. At .7 m. pass airplane beacon. Descend by wood road, turn E (sharp R) on path and soon N (sharp L) at hemlocks, continuing to first crossing of Baldwin Parkway at .9 m. Follow path, inclining to R on survey line (yellow markers), and continue through woods and laurel, turning L from survey line and crossing Parkway again at 1.2 m.

NORTHERN RANGE

(U.S.G.S. quadrangles: New Haven, Mount Carmel)

Trail now follows western cliffs, with excellent views, more and more of the N outlook opening up as ridge slowly tends to E. Cross parking area. At 4.4 m. cross Baldwin Parkway a third time. (Fine view to E.) Continue N to hogback with more good outlooks. Cross Parkway again at 4.8 m. and reascend western cliffs at 4.9 m. with attractive view of West River valley. Trail now swings NE through attractive woodlands, crossing Parkway at 5.3 m. and, after circling eastern cliffs (views), makes a final crossing of the Parkway to N outlook at 5.9 m. (Gaylord Mt. in foreground). At 6.2 m. trail ascends steeply .1 m. to join Quinnipiac Trail at Sanford Notch at 6.3 m.

SANFORD FEEDER

(U.S.G.S. quadrangle: Mount Carmel)

The Sanford Feeder is approximately .6 m. long and connects Brooks Rd., Bethany with the Regicides Trail. It follows an abandoned town road through varied terrain, passing abandoned farmsteads, crossing a small wetland, finally ascending parallel to a talus slope. It joins the Regicides Trail near the junction of the Regicides and Quinnipiac Trails.

SALMON RIVER TRAIL

(U.S.G.S. quadrangle: Moodus)

The Salmon River Trail consists of a system of two loop trails, a N loop and a S loop, both of which begin at Day Pond State Park in the Westchester section of Colchester and are located within the Park and adjacent Salmon River State Forest. See map Salmon River Trail.

SALMON RIVER TRAIL

NORTH LOOP

The N Loop of the Salmon River Trail leaves the road and parking area from the N side of the dam, follows an old wood road in a NE direction about 100 yds., leaves this wood road sharply L. The trail descends the hill NW for about 100 yds., crosses a utility easement and continues along the N side of Pond Brook for about ¼ m. The N Loop proceeds uphill through a laurel stand and across an electric utility easement. The trail proceeds in a broad loop through predominantly deciduous woods, gradually bearing L to join Day Pond Rd. at about 2 m. Here the hiker has the options of: (a) proceeding about 30 yds. up the road to join the South Loop, (b) proceeding up the hill on Day Pond Rd. to reenter Day Pond Park, or (c) proceeding down Day Pond Rd. to view river at site of former Salmon River bridge.

SOUTH LOOP

The S Loop of the Salmon River Trail leaves the park road several yds. from the dam at Day Pond Park. The trail proceeds 30 yds. W, crosses Day Pond Rd. and bears sharply R after crossing the remnants of an old stone wall. The trail proceeds W for approx. .3 m. to a large isolated glacial erratic. The trail continues W, crosses a small brook and ascends gradually to the utility easement at the crest of a hill. (Good view of the Salmon River valley.) The trail crosses the easement, turns sharply R, descends the hill, mostly N, initially through deciduous woods, then through dense hemlock stands. At 1.5 m. the trail crosses an electric utility easement, then continues through dense hemlock and shortly reaches Day Pond Brook, parallels an old stone wall, crosses the brook and ascends sharply E to intersect Day Pond Rd. Connection can be made from the S Loop to the N Loop by proceeding about 30 yds. to the L along Day Pond Rd. The total distance is about 2 m.

COMSTOCK BRIDGE CONNECTOR

The S Loop of the Salmon River Trail connects with the Comstock bridge connector immediately W of the intersection of the S Loop with the pipeline easement. The trail proceeds downslope, passing an overlook of the river valley and arrives high on the bank of the river. Bearing L, the trail follows the river high on the bank with a good view of the river, descends through a pine plantation, follows the river bank and finally arrives at the E end of Comstock bridge. (Distance approx. 2 m.)

SHENIPSIT TRAIL

With the exception of a gap of about 11 m. between Bolton Center Rd. in Bolton and Crystal Lake Rd. in Ellington and an occasional short bypass by rd., this is a through trail from the Cobalt section of East Hampton to the Mass. line via the Meshomasic and Shenipsit State Forests. Six sections covering about 29 m. are now in existence. See maps Shenipsit Trail, numbers 1, 2, 4.

GREAT HILL POND TO NEW LONDON TURNPIKE

(U.S.G.S. quadrangles: Middle Haddam, Glastonbury)

From the intersection of Rts. 66 and 151 in Cobalt, go N .1 m., turn R at "Y" intersection, and at .8 m. turn R at second "Y" intersection. Proceed additional .5 m. to intersection with gravel rd.

Leaving the rd., trail heads NW through woods and soon starts climbing. Getting steeper, trail heads W and then NW and ascends quite steeply to jct. on top of Great Hill ridge at .43 m. (White-blazed trail leads L .8 m. to spectacular lookout over Great Hill Pond and Connecticut River.)

Turning R, main trail continues along crest of ridge (town line between Portland and East Hampton). (At .59 m. side trail leads R to lookout.) Continuing NNE trail joins tote rd. at 1.77 m. Turning sharp R (E) trail soon joins another tote rd. continuing E downgrade, then swings NE, joins another tote rd. at 1.93 m. and comes to Forest Service dirt rd. at 1.96 m.

After crossing the service rd. (Woodchopper Rd.), the trail proceeds past the remnant of a small quarry and joins a wood rd. for about .25 m., bearing to the L down slope through the woods, crossing a small brook and then in about .2 m. crossing a larger brook. The trail proceeds past an attractive cascade (in wet season) and in about 50 yds. bears R to ascend Bald Hill. Continuing NNE, trail ascends and reaches Bald Hill at 2.9 m. After descending steeply, trail makes an easy descent to bottom of sag to tote rd. Turning R (E), trail follows this tote rd. to jct. with another tote rd. at 3.59 m. Here straight ahead off the trail is located "Biscuit Rock."

Turning L (N) on tote rd., trail meets a tote rd. at 4.29 m., skirts pine forest and an additional tote rd. at 4.95 m. Turning R, trail follows this tote rd. NE, passes small fire pond and comes to double blaze at 5.93 m. (Straight ahead the tote rd. descends .5 m. to jct. of White Birch and Portland Rds., 1.25 m. W of Rt. 2 via Portland Rd.)

Trail turns sharp L from tote rd., heading N. After slight descent, trail turns E, crosses three small brooks and at 6.57 m. turns L. Trail swings NE, then E and joins another tote rd. at 6.84 m. (Tote rd. R leads S .32 m. to jct. of White Birch and Portland Rds.) Turning L, tote rd. is followed E past field, then descends N. At 7.64 m. trail leaves rd. and heads N and NE through woods and reaches twin boulders at 7.9 m. Descending steeply NE for 110 yds., trail swings N through laurel at foot of high cliff and comes to Rt. 2 *(limited access)* at 8.16 m. (2.4 m. E of Exit 10 at Rt. 83.)

To continue N from Rt. 2, roads can be followed on foot. First go N from the Shenipsit Trail on a white blazed trail to the end of Dickinson Rd. (See Map No. 1.) Cross Rt. 2 on the Wassuc Rd. overpass and turn S on Toll Gate Rd. Continue S from turn-around on old rd. to jct. with Shenipsit Trail.

Since Rt. 2 is a limited access hwy., the following suggestions are made to avoid the hazards of parking beside the hwy. or crossing on foot in order to start a hike at that point. To proceed *N* from Rt. 2, take the Thompson Rd. Exit from the W-bound lane, turn R immediately on Toll Gate Rd. Park at turnaround on Toll Gate Rd. and walk to top of ridge on old rd. which parallels N side of hwy. Watch for hwy. trail sign on N side of Rt. 2.

To proceed *S* on the trail, turn R from the E-bound lane of Rt. 2 at Manchester Rd. Exit (Rt. 83). Turn L immediately on Old New London Tnpke.; turn R on Country Club Rd. then L on

Mott Hill Rd. and proceed to Dickinson Rd. Cars can be left at end of pavement on Mott Hill or Dickinson Rd. Watch for white blazes which indicate access trails to Shenipsit Trail from either rd.

ROUTE 2 TO HEBRON AVE.

(U.S.G.S. quadrangles: Glastonbury, Marlborough)

Leaving Rt. 2, the trail heads NE, crosses a small brook at .14 m. Now heading NNE, trail ascends, bears R over small ridge, and after descending through small sag, heads E over bare rock to top of ridge at .29 m. (view).

Turning sharp L along ridge, trail descends gradually and joins tote rd. at .44 m. Then climbing ENE through laurel, route continues along a tote rd. N and NE. After crossing brook at 1.05 m., trail passes at 1.18 m. old stone walls of abandoned farmstead. At 1.28 m., trail veers L away from brook, swings E slightly and passes through Kongscut Trust property. Trail proceeds to edge of hill for view of Hartford, then turns sharply to R through large laurel stand and finally bears L to join unpaved Windham Rd.

Trail turns R from Windham Rd. at 2.29 m. and heads E on a tote rd. Bearing R at fork, trail descends gradually and crosses brook at 2.52 m. Continuing E, trail eventually swings N, and then at about 2.8 m. it bears E over ridge past large rock and on to bluff overlooking Flat Brook. It turns N and gradually descends to W bank of Flat Brook, which it follows N. The trail gradually steepens to attain a utility easement, which it follows E about 50 yd. After crossing Flat Brook, the trail follows the E bank upstream through a stand of trees and along the edge of an orchard.

When the trail reaches a paved access road to a development, it crosses Flat Brook to woods on the W bank. It continues N through the woods to a dam at the S end of a shallow pond. From there it goes NW on a well-worn foot trail to Diamond Lake Rd.

After crossing Diamond Lake Rd., the trail goes up the E side of Flat Brook, through woods and past a holding pond of a development. The trail continues through woods and an orchard and along a dike of the holding pond. Then it passes through a narrow corridor between two houses and reaches Hebron Ave. It crosses to the N side and goes L a short distance to Hill St. at about 5 m. from Rt. 2.

HEBRON AVE. TO HIGHLAND PARK

(U.S.G.S. quadrangles: Marlborough, Rockville)

Leaving Hebron Ave. (Rt. 94, 7.4 m. E of Glastonbury center) the trail heads N on Hill St. At .14 m. the trail enters the woods on the left, following an old tote road along the edge of a field and climbing gradually to the top of a ridge at .34 m. The trail continues through the woods (passing under power lines at .53 m.) and reaches a large glacial boulder and a trail junction at .75 m.

[The John Tom Hill connector (red/blue) goes to the right .44 m. to Birch Mtn. Rd. The trail makes a step descent and at .15 m. crosses a brook. The trail then passes under the power lines and continues through the woods to Birch Mtn. Rd. .1 m. N of the Glastonbury Fire Tower.]

Descending N it goes past swamp on dam just before crossing tote rd. at 1.31 m. (Birch Mtn. Rd., R, .8 m.) and climbs ridge to Pine Ledge at 1.52 m. (views). Turning R at 1.55 m., trail soon reaches top of ridge, turns L and descends N through a sag and climbs to Garnet Ledge, at 1.85 m., studded with tiny garnets. In about 50 yds. trail descends abruptly N, crossing over bare rocks and an old dam just before crossing brook at 2.04 m. Now heading NW, trail continues over easy grades and leaves open woods at 2.32 m. After crossing a bushy meadow, trail crosses Roaring Brook at 2.41 m. and comes to dirt Coopers Sawmill Rd. at 2.56 m. (.3 m. S of crossing, a red-on-blue blazed trail on the W side leads .1 m. to large glacial boulder and then .2 m. back to the Shenipsit Trail.)

Crossing rd. and continuing NW, trail climbs the ridge (trail from glacial boulder enters at 2.70 m.) and then heads N to jct. with a yellow blazed trail at 3.48 m. (This leads 1.3 m. to Camp Merriwood, Manchester Girl Scouts.) Continuing straight ahead trail enters tote rd. at 3.64 m. and comes to jct. at 3.92 m. (Trail L leads to Camp Merriwood at 1.55 m. It heads W and SW, skirts a swamp and makes a T connection with another tote rd. at .25 m. Tote rd. L leads .7 m. S to another tote rd. which is the above-mentioned blazed trail. To the R this leads .6 m. to Camp Merriwood on Gardner St., Manchester and to the L .7 m. back to the Shenipsit Trail.)

Bearing R at jct., Shenipsit Trail continues N on tote rd. crossing Highland Park Loop (blue and yellow blazes) at 4.06 m. to Lookout Jct. at 4.22 m. (Trail L with yellow-on-blue blazes leads .7 m. to Birch Mtn. Lookout (744 ft.) with excellent W view. Straight ahead at Lookout Jct., yellow-on-blue tote rd. crosses cinder rd. in .15 m., soon forks R and at another jct. continues on R fork to Highland Park Springs at .72 m.)

Turning R at Lookout Jct., Shenipsit Trail leaves tote rd. and proceeds to another jct. with the Highland Park Loop, then heads N along rock ledges above site of old granite quarry, turns R, descends across tote rd. (part of Highland Park Loop leading L to spring at .55 m.) and reaches cinder rd. at 4.5 m. Trail follows rd. L for 100 yds. then turns sharply R, climbing gradually through laurel stand. Reaching top of ridge at 4.8 m. trail heads E, crosses tote rd. at 4.96 m. and descends to Birch Mtn. Rd. at 5.08 m. (Parking).

HIGHLAND PARK TO BOLTON CENTER ROAD

(U.S.G.S. quadrangle: Rockville)

Trail follows Birch Mt. Rd. and at .22 m. crosses Birch Mt. Brook. Then swinging SW, the trail follows a tote rd., bears L up grade at .33 m. and passes corner of large field with good view. Then descending to cross an open stretch, the trail enters woods again and rejoins old route at .51 m.

Turning L along pine ridge, trail reaches height of land at .53 m. After descending, the trail climbs gradually, and after turning L, reaches Carter St. at .71 m. Crossing Carter St. trail follows AGT pipeline right-of-way to the N. At .95 m. trail enters woods to L and shortly crosses stream. At 1.1 m. trail reaches Camp Meeting Rd. opposite Finley St. Follow Finley St. and turn R on East Hillcrest Rd. at 2.44 m. to reach jct. of U.S. 6 (Rt. 44) and Bolton Center Rd. (Rt. 85) at 2.89 m.

SHENIPSIT TRAIL

U.S. 6 TO CRYSTAL LAKE ROAD

This section will form a possible future extension of the trail from U.S. 6 to Mile Hill Rd., and thence to Crystal Lake Rd. The map for this section will be Shenipsit Trail Map No. 3

CRYSTAL LAKE ROAD TO SOAPSTONE MOUNTAIN

(U.S.G.S. quadrangle: Ellington)

The start of the trail is reached from Rockville by going 3 m. N on Rt. 83 to Crystal Lake Rd. (Rt. 140) then 1.4 m. E to Lake Bonair and Hopkins Rd. where blue blazes begin at Hopkins Rd. sign.

The trail follows Hopkins Rd. W .12 m. and turns R onto tote rd. State Forest begins here.

Leaving Hopkins Rd., the trail follows tote rd. N .44 m., turns NW, crosses a brook, and joins another tote rd. at .51 m. Turning R, this tote rd. is followed N along height of land, and turns L (W) at 1.22 m. At 1.27 m. the trail turns R (N). Trail soon becomes a footpath, passing forest boundary marker at 1.3 m. and enters private land. At 1.45 m. trail meets another tote rd. Turning L, this tote rd. soon turns N again and joins Porter Rd. at 1.66 m. (An abandoned town rd. which provides access to the Shenipsit Trail.)

The trail follows Porter Rd. L and at 1.84 m. turns N, sharp R on tote rd. At 2.1 m. trail again enters and remains in the Shenipsit State Forest to Soapstone Mtn. Soapstone Rd. is reached at 2.87 m.

Crossing Soapstone Rd. and proceeding NNW the trail climbs to a lookout at 3.06 m. The trail now heads NE and crosses dirt Parker Rd. (an access rd. from Rt. 83) that crosses Soapstone Rd. about 50 yds. R. at 3.51 m.

The trail continues on a tote rd. and soon branches L, crosses another tote rd. and zigzags up a ridge at 3.59 m. Proceeding NE, the trail later turns N and joins a tote rd. at 3.78 m. Turning R, the tote rd. is followed to 3.84 m. where the trail branches R and soon climbs to the W summit of Soapstone Mtn. at 4.01 m. (El. 930′).

Continuing N and then NE, trail soon makes abrupt zigzag descent to tote rd. and in another 100 yds. comes out at lower Soapstone Mtn. picnic area on Soapstone Rd. at 4.3 m. Turning L, a tote rd. is followed to a R turn at 4.46 m. (The tote rd. straight ahead, marked with yellow blazes, is the bypass around peak of Soapstone Mtn. and rejoins the Shenipsit Trail in .4 m.)

The trail, now a footpath, proceeds ESE up the steep cone of Soapstone Mtn. and reaches Somers fire tower on summit at 4.79 m. (El. 1075'). (Graded path S leads to upper picnic area and parking on Soapstone Rd. A short distance down rd. a trail on L leads past old soapstone quarry for which the mountain was named.)

SOAPSTONE MOUNTAIN TO OLD COUNTY ROAD

(U.S.G.S. quadrangle: Ellington)

Trail branches L from telephone line a few yds. N of tower and descends steep cone of Soapstone Mtn. to tote rd. at .29 m. (See bypass above.) Trail turns R, crosses Gulf Rd. at .42 m., becomes a footpath, and reaches tote rd. at .64 m. (R .1 m. to Sodom Rd.) Trail follows tote rd. to fork at .91 m. At 1.13 m. the trail divides: main trail R goes over rocky promontory; trail L skirts it to rejoin main route at 1.18 m. Tote rd. is reached at 1.35 m. (Sodom Rd. .1 m R)

The trail turns R (E) to Sodom Rd. at 1.59 m., where it turns L (N) on rd. to Rt. 190 at 1.92 m. It goes L .1 m. to Galbraith Rd., where it turns R and follows the rd. N to fork at 2.23 m. Trail turns L entering woods and climbing to high ground, descends and crosses Lievre Brook at 2.58 m., reaching a low ridge at 2.68 m. Descending gradually, the trail crosses a tributary of Lievre Brook and at 2.97 m. reaches Old County Rd., the present northern teminus of the Shenipsit Trail.

(L this dirt rd., passable by cars, leads .75 m. to Rt. 190 about 1 m. W of the Shenipsit Trail crossing. R it leads .75 m. to a State Forest dirt rd. Turning R on this rd. it is .6 m. to Galbraith Rd. and R another .2 m. to Rt. 190.)

SLEEPING GIANT TRAILS

(U.S.G.S. quadrangles: Mount Carmel, Wallingford)

From the New Haven Harbor the outstanding landmark on the skyline to the N is the silhouette of the Sleeping Giant, lying on his *back*, *feet* to the E, *head* to the W with his prominent rocky *chin* thrust upward to the sky. On it there are distant views from the rocky crags, remote quiet woods, pleasant pine groves and mountain brooks with mossy cascades.

To help you enjoy exploration, The Sleeping Giant Park Association has constructed an interconnected trail system. About 30 miles of hiking trails lead around, up, over and along the Giant to the most interesting places in the 1477 acres of this State Park. For a description of the Quinnipiac Trail within the Park, see p. 76. See map Trails on the Sleeping Giant.

WHITE TRAIL

The eastern terminus of the White Trail is at the point where the Yellow, Orange, Violet and Green Trails join. It forms the S side of the Blue-White circuit of all the major peaks. Its white paint blazes lead over the *right lower left leg*, *right knee* (with good views N and S) very steeply down over the rocks to the base of the cliff of this *knee* and up onto the *right thigh* to Bare Rock, with sweeping S views. It passes the remains of a tumbled down stone house and along the *upper right thigh,* across the *waist* and up onto the rocky slabs of the *left shoulder,* with broad views to distant horizons and, close by, the great rocky wall of the massive *chin*. A winding downward trail leads back to the picnic area rd. Total distance 2.8 m. Blue-White Trail circuit 5.6 m.

VIOLET-YELLOW-ORANGE-GREEN TRAILS

These four E-W trails are less strenuous, and change elevation less frequently or violently. They can be enjoyed singly or in a circuit combination with any one of the other trails. The W terminus of each is the picnic area rd. The eastern termini are E of the *right foot* at a surfaced rd., which can be reached from Whitney Ave. by traveling about 2 m. E on Mt. Carmel Ave. and N up Chestnut La. to the second sharp turn.

The Violet Trail from the picnic area rd. goes along Mill River and the edge of the Old Axle Shop Pond, across the lower quarry floor, over some foundations of old quarry buildings and the abandoned quarry ramp rd. to the N side of the Giant's *head*, an elevation half way up the mountain. The trail continues E, more or less on contour, for the length of the N side of the Giant. The entire trip is through wooded country, shaded in summer but with N views when the leaves are off. Year 'round NW views are provided from the rocky ledges on the lower slopes of his *left hand*. Down from these and around to the N of the *left knee* brings one to the E end at 3.2 m.

The Yellow Trail makes a good return trip W from the E end of the Violet Trail. It, too, winds along pretty much on contour, half way up the S side of the Giant. This trail also is shady, with outlooks from two rocky spots on the *right thigh*. Several short, steep switchbacks lead down to the last gradual sloping return under ancient hemlocks at the Hexagon Trail intersection. A level stretch on the Tower Path leads to the picnic area rd. Total distance 2.2 m. Violet-Yellow circuit 5.4 m.

The Orange Trail, leaving the picnic area rd. and going E, uses much of the old Heaton Trail in its climb around the SE side of the Giant's *chest* (vistas SE). It crosses the *waist* and follows the N side of the *right leg* with views over the Inner Mountain Valley. It joins the Violet, Yellow, Green and White Trails at its eastern terminus, at 2.4 m.

The Green Trail's eastern terminus is where the Violet, Yellow, Orange and White Trails come together. It follows old wood rds. W and passes through the Inner Mountain Valley, across the *waist*, and finally emerges on the rocky ledges of the *right shoulder* (views). Total distance about 2 m.

DIAMOND-HEXAGON-TRIANGLE-CIRCLE-SQUARE RED TRAILS

Five N-S trails through notches connect Mt. Carmel Ave. on the S with Tuttle Ave. or Mansion Rd. on the N, crossing all the E-W trails. The Diamond Trail more or less parallels Mill River and crosses the floor of the abandoned trap rock quarry W of the *head*. Distance .7 m.

The Hexagon Trail climbs across the *neck* under the impressive stone cliff *chin*. Distance: S of blue .7 m.; N of blue .4 m. Total 1.1 m.

The Triangle Trail is the belt across the *waist* and has some steep climbs on both the N and S sides. Distance: S of blue .6 m.; N of blue .5 m. Total 1.1 m.

The Circle Trail uses much of the old Dickerman Carriage Rd. on its climb up the S slope. Passing below the cliffs of the *right knee*, it goes down the N side along the banks of the brook which drains the Inner Mountain Valley, passing through laurel, hemlock and beech along a delightful stream descending over mossy rocks and eventually down a series of cascades through a fifty foot deep gorge. Distance: S of blue 1.1 m.; N of blue .8 m. Total 1.9 m.

The Square Trail makes an interesting traverse just E of the *knees*. Distance: S of blue 1.1 m.; N of blue .5 m. Total 1.6 m.

These five red trails provide worthwhile trips in themselves, but are frequently used as feeders or crossovers in conjunction with other trails to provide loop walks of almost any desired length. The map also shows several other crossovers.

Nature Trail

This trail starts at the bottom of the Tower Path. The distinctive pine tree markings will take you on about an hour's walk. The numbered stations are described in a guide booklet available free from the Park Manager.

Tower Path

The wide gravel Tower Path is maintained by the State. It winds in easy grades from the Park entrance up through the *neck* and along the north of the *chest* to the Stone Tower. Total distance 1.6 m.

Horse Trail

A Horseback Trail, painted with U blazes, extends from Chestnut La. to Tuttle Ave. Hikers please note: the Horse Trail is designated for horses only. During the winter, a large part of the Horse Trail is utilized as a cross country ski trail, blazed with temporary markings. Maps are available at the trail heads.

Sleeping Giant Information

Drinking water, rest rooms, telephone, picnic tables and camping spots are all available at Park Headquarters.

Fires and overnight camping are restricted to

this area and the rugged Cascade Primitive Area, where special advanced permission is required for small camping groups under experienced adult leaders.

The map shows unblazed trails for those wishing greater variety.

Motorized vehicles are not permitted on the trails.

SUNNY VALLEY FOUNDATION TRAILS

(U.S.G.S. quadrangles: New Milford, Roxbury)

The Sunny Valley Foundation properties in Bridgewater consist of nearly 1500 acres of both open space and farmland. The Foundation, organized to revitalize New England agriculture, has built and maintains this trail system as part of its multiple-use land management plan. See map Sunny Valley Foundation Trails.

The White, Red and Yellow Trails are through trails, leading from one parcel of land to others. White is the longest. It runs from the Bridgewater Town Park on Lake Lillinonah to the S end of the Iron Ore Hill parcel on Iron Ore Hill Rd.

The Red Trail intersects the White Trail at both ends and also doubles with the White Trail near the bridge at Benson Rd. The Yellow Trail is an E-W route between Rocky Hill and Silica Mine Hill, and the Blue Trails serve as short connectors between the major trails and offer many opportunities for circular walks of varying lengths.

These trails exist through the courtesy of the Foundation and several private landowners. Hikers are invited to use them with respect for private property in accordance with the following rules: stay on marked paths and keep dogs on leashes in the vicinity of houses and farm pastures.

Prohibited throughout: motor vehicles, including snowmobiles and all-terrain vehicles; cutting of live or dead trees; fires, hunting; radios and tape players. Destroy no vegetation, respect rare flowers, and leave no litter.

Detailed maps are available from the Foundation office. Write or call:

> Sunny Valley Foundation
> 4 Sunny Valley Lane
> New Milford, CT 06776
> (203) 355-3715

TUNXIS TRAIL

The southern section of the Tunxis (from Southington to New Hartford) is, in general, a network system so that closed circuit walks may be made. It is divided into 3 parts with a 7-mile break in the vicinity of Bristol, and a 2-mile break between Rt. 4 and Hotchkiss Rd., Burlington.

South of Bristol there are 15.27 miles; between Bristol and Rt. 4, 34.94 miles; and between Hotchkiss Rd. and the Rt. 44 bridge at Satan's Kingdom Gorge in New Hartford, 11.3 miles. The trails are primarily woodland paths with only 6 outstanding viewpoints. Exceptional features are one of the steepest miles in the Connecticut Trail System; a historical landmark, Tory Den; the unique and rough Mile of Ledges; a box ravine known as Devil's Kitchen; and Norton Outlook with a 50-mile, 180° view.

See map, Tunxis Trail, Wolcott to Satan's Kingdom. For a description of the northern section, see p. 113.

South of Bristol

(U.S.G.S. quadrangles: Southington, Bristol)

MAINLINE TRAIL

0.00 Trail begins at corner of Whitman and Mt. Vernon Rds. on the W side of Southington, near the Wolcott town line. (Parking). Climb gravel rd.

0.20 Stay L of Southington Sportmans' Assoc. Club House and rifle range. Be careful on Sunday a.m. to get an "all clear."

0.27 Trail takes abrupt L and follows archery range service road.

0.62 Climb small steep bank; then go L on Whitman Rd. (a non-maintained town rd.).

1.49 Trail emerges into clearing beside Roaring Brook. Bear L and follow the Westside Service Rd.

1.58 Jct. with Stonehouse Trail. (Stonehouse Trail L.) Continue on Westside Service Rd.

2.18 Jct. with Woodtick Trail. (Woodtick Trail L.)

2.25 Cross old stone culvert and prepare to leave rd. R upgrade and shortly to high tension wires. Cross and descend to Old Alcott Rd.

2.58 Turn sharp L onto North-South Rd. (Lady's slippers in season.)

2.73 Leave rd. abruptly R and climb.
3.04 Libby's Lump. (South Arm of Compounce Loop R.)
3.29 North-South Road N, climb gradually near the summit (wooded) of Compounce Mt.
3.72 Narrow foot path leads N and in about 100 yds. bears R, downgrade.
3.93 Jct. with the North Arm of Compounce Loop. (North Arm of Compounce Loop R.)
4.15 Trail turns L along wood rd.
4.26 Sharp turn R, skirting a pasture.
4.32 Turn square L. Private Pond of the Bristol Fish & Game Club visible through trees R.
4.59 Emerge onto Beecher Rd.—end of the Mainline.

[Prior to development, the Main Line continued by skirting to S side of Jacklin Lake and down South Mt. N, across Terryville Rd., following close to Clark Ave. and the RR spur to the Old Marsh Reservoir where the Mainline now restarts.]

WOODTICK TRAIL

This trail provides access to the Roaring Brook Reservoir area from Wolcott, leaving Woodtick Rd. between the height-of-land and a high tension line about .75 m. S of Rt. 69. Entering dry, open woods it follows a fine old wood road, level at first but then dropping quite steeply to Beecher Rd., (gravel) at .38 m. Five hundred ft. from Woodtick Rd. just before the steep downgrade, the historic Alcott Cemetery is passed on the right. Louisa May Alcott's forebears are interred here. Trail bears R on this road for about 400 ft. and just beyond the high tension line turns squarely L into the woods immediately crossing a small stream. The trail gradually slants away from the powerline, passes an old cellar hole, and at .55 m. turns sharply R along an old wood road. Avoiding a swampy area it then climbs a long hill, the N slope of Southington Mt. As the old road levels off, the Woodtick Trail turns L. (The Stonehouse Trail continues straight ahead.) The trail now descends slightly, crosses another small stream, and bears L a few yds. on another wood road. Then it swings R and follows a low, ledgy ridge from which it descends rather abruptly to the Westside Service Rd. Total distance: 1.55 m.

STONEHOUSE TRAIL

This woodland path continues straight ahead where the Woodtick Trail makes its fourth sharp turn. It continues S along the NE slope of Southington Mt., and in about .4 m., near the ruins of an old stone house, turns acutely L. For most of the next mile it follows an old road, leaving it just short of Roaring Brook Reservoir. The trail terminates at the Westside Service Rd. at 1.26 m.

SOUTH ARM OF COMPOUNCE LOOP

This trail begins at the cul-de-sac of a rd. named Panthorne Trail. The trail accesses the Compounce Loop Crossover and ends where it intersects the Tunxis Mainline Trail. Lake Compounce and Compounce Mt. are named for John Compound, who signed the original Mattatuck (Waterbury) deed of 1674.

From Bristol S, Lake Ave. becomes Mt. Vernon Rd. and Panthorne Trail is the first R in Southington.

0.00 Enter cul-de-sac, continue straight and enter woods.
0.10 Sharp turn L and ascend. (Abandoned rt. to Lake Compounce continues straight, crossing brook.)
0.20 L along a shelf crossing 2 small brooks.
0.46 R onto an old rd. for a few hundred ft.
0.50 Jct. with Compounce Loop Crossover Trail. Climb out to the L and continue along the steep escarpment of Compounce Mt.
0.91 Madsen's Mound with limited views.
1.03 Jct. with Mainline Trail. Cross Mainline to rock face known as Libby's Lump.

NORTH ARM OF COMPOUNCE LOOP

The North Arm begins on the N side of Cussgutter Brook where it crosses Lake Ave. Parking. This trail is the starting point to also access the Bristol–Lake Compounce Trail and the Compounce Cascade Trail.

0.00 Cussgutter Parking Area. Head W up gradual slope, along wide wood rd.
0.07 Veer L onto wood trail.
0.13 "Cussgutter Jct." (The Bristol–Lake Compounce Trail begins here by continuing straight.) Proceed sharp L down to the brook, cross, and climb bank to old wood

rd. Turn R and climb steeply for about 100 yds., then more moderately, the way eroded and resembling a dry brook bed.

0.38 At prominent white birch, continue straight onto old wood rd. trace with the grade lessening. (Avoid severely eroded old rt. leading R.)

0.52 Regain the original North Arm rt. (Just ahead 50 ft. the Julian's Rock Loop leaves R.)

0.78 "The Gateway" (Compounce Loop Crossover leaves L.) (Julian's Rock Link leaves at a hairpin R.) Turn square R and descend gradually crossing a branch of Cussgutter Brook. Climb gradually along an old wood rd.

1.19 Jct. with Mainline Trail.

COMPOUNCE LOOP CROSSOVER

This trail links the North and South Arms of the Compounce Loop near its midsection and offers a shorter closed circuit walk from Lake Compounce, and access to two scenic viewpoints.

Leaving the South Arm of the Compounce Loop .67 m. from the lake, the Compounce Loop Crossover generally follows a woodroad trace upgrade rather steeply and gains a natural ramp on the E face of the mountain. At the end of this it bears R, crosses a tiny brook (usually dry), passes over two ledges and while passing a third arrives at a junction at .3 m. A dead-end spur leads straight ahead for 30 yds. to Compounce Outlook with a view of lake below.

At the junction the main trail turns L, passes across a minor depression and shortly begins the steep climb to Norton Outlook. At first it slabs the mountain but then makes a direct ascent up a minor ravine. Nearing the ledge it swings in an arc to the R and then switchbacks up the ledge to its summit at .5 m.

On a clear day Mt. Tom near Northampton, Mass., is visible as is Long Island beyond the Sound.

The Compounce Loop Crossover descends a ledgy ridge N via several switchbacks. Gaining a col it bears R and descends steeply, then swings L and into a continuation of the original woodroad trace it was following. In 50 yds. it passes the sheer rock face of a little cliff and terminates at the North Arm of the Compounce Loop at .7 m.

JULIAN'S ROCK LOOP

This scenic loop leads E from "The Gateway" regaining the North Arm .28 m. downgrade toward Lake Compounce. It provides easy access to a ledge with a view almost as expansive as that from Norton Outlook.

At first descending slightly, it then climbs over a ledgy knoll and then ascends a backbone of rock to the viewpoint at .12 m. Turning somewhat more northeasterly it passes into a pine grove where the Compounce Cascade Trail diverges L at .19 m. (Bristol, 3.01 m; Bristol-Compounce Trail at foot of mountain, .86 m.) Then passing through low bushy growth (good views) it descends the steepest pitch on the Southern Tunxis, 42% grade, regaining the North Arm at .35 mile. (Total length, .35 m.)

BRISTOL-LAKE COMPOUNCE TRAIL

This trail, running between South St., Bristol and the Lake Compounce Amusement Park, is frequently used as a hiking route to the lake.

The Bristol-Lake Compounce Trail leaves the S side of Mountain Rd., about 150 ft. E of Downs St. It climbs abruptly along an old road, L at fork, and climbs steeply into a high tension line corridor at .8 m.

The high tension line is followed S and at .49 m. the trail gains the top of an old dump. Continuing S along a jeep road it bears L into mature forest near a deep ravine. Swinging R it climbs to a wood road trace, turning L onto it.

The wood road leads up a long hill and at its summit the trail swings R and climbs directly upward beside a big rock outcrop. After some switchbacks it bears L along an old road that runs along the E side of South Mt. This is the Old Emerson Rd., the stagecoach route between Bristol and Waterbury in pre-Revolutionary times. At 1.34 m., just short of a high tension line, there is a good ledge overlooking E. Bristol (L 50 yds.) The old road continues along the side of the mountain and at 2.02 m. crosses a brook (campsite on L). Climbing moderately the trail leaves the old road, turning squarely L at 2.08 m. (Julian's Rock Link continues straight ahead. Julian's Rock, 1 m.).

Now the trail descends a broad ridge, crossing two small brooks, and joins a tractor road at 2.45

m. At 2.67 m. it bears R along another tractor road and descends to Cussgutter Brook which it reaches at 2.76 m. (Compounce Cascade Trail diverges R. Julian's Rock, .93 m.).

The trail now bears L closely following the brook's N bank and reaches Cussgutter Jct. at 2.85 m. (North Arm of Compounce Loop leaves R.) Continuing straight it arrives at Cussgutter Parking Area at 2.98 m.

COMPOUNCE CASCADE TRAIL

This trail follows Cussgutter Brook for about .5 m. and then climbs onto Julian's Rock. With 6 brook crossings, it is not a good highwater trail, and ascent is more desirable than descent due to its rocky nature. Since its opening it has become a very popular route.

For the first 250 ft., this trail climbs moderately on the N side of the brook. It then crosses and almost immediately recrosses the stream at .6 m. The hiker is now at the foot of The Chute where the stream drops over 300 ft. in a series of cascades. At .17 m. the top of The Chute is reached in a canyon called Purgatory. Thereafter the trail again crosses and recrosses the stream gaining a woodroad trace at .22 m. This follows a much more gradual route to the forking of the West and South Branches of Cussgutter Brook at .48 m. (Julian's Rock Link diverges, R. Bristol, 2.73 m.)

The trail now crosses the West Branch, and then in about 50 yds., the South Branch. It then climbs steeply up Suicide Hill which is topped by a difficult ledge (Limited N and W views).

After crossing a step it climbs again, steeply at first and then more gradually and terminates at the Julian's Rock Loop at .86 m.; Julian's Rock, R, .7 m.

JULIAN'S ROCK LINK

This trail creates a direct route from Bristol to the ledges on Compounce Mt. Leaving the Bristol-Compounce Trail 2.08 m. from Mountain Rd., it continues straight ahead, slabbing the mountainside. It crosses two minor ridges separated by a little brook and then descends more noticeably crossing another drainage trough that is usually wet. Climbing again it gains a plateau of oak. It descends steeply from this but in steps, to the Compounce Cascade Trail. (Total length, .65 m.).

Bristol to Rt. 4, Burlington

(U.S.G.S. quadrangles: Thomaston, Bristol, Torrington, Collinsville)

This section of the Southern Tunxis consists of 3 roughly parallel routes that branch just N of Old Marsh (#7) Reservoir and converge again just S of Rt. 4. with some links between the routes. To aid in route-finding a color-coding system has been devised to avoid confusion. The blazes of the Mainline remain all blue but other trails have small contrasting dots: white, yellow, orange, green, pink, red, or black in the middle of the blue blaze.

THE MAINLINE

After the break at Bristol the Southern Tunxis begins again just W of the dam of Old Marsh (#7) Reservoir, leaving the N side of Marsh Rd., just within the Town of Plymouth. From this point there are no further breaks to Rt. 4 in Burlington.

Leaving Marsh Rd., the trail passes between backyards and the shore of the reservoir for 100 yds., then enters a pine forest. It travels between E. Church Rd. and the W shore of the reservoir through woods to a "T" junction (Old Marsh Jct.) at .8 m. The White Dot Route leads L from this junction toward E. Plymouth Rd., while the Mainline turns R along an old road toward Tory Den. The road climbs gradually, then descends and crosses one of the reservoir's principal feeder streams. After crossing a small swamp, the Tunxis curves L and climbs gradually to a junction at 1.4 m. (Yellow Dot Route continues straight to historic Tory Den and eventually to Johnnycake Rd.) The Mainline turns R along the Mile of Ledges, the roughest part of the Southern Tunxis. The first .5 m. is one big ledge after another, and in one instance the trail goes through the middle of one. The trail continues up and down and crosses Garnet Brook which justifies its name. Near its end, the high bank of a small pond, a haven for migrating water fowl, is followed. At 2.99 m., the Mainline turns R along paved Greer Rd. (L on Greer Rd. leads to Yellow Dot Route).

At 3.19 m. W. Chippens Hill Rd. is crossed and the Mainline continues straight through a private yard via the Hemenway Lookout Trail. It descends slightly, skirting a field, then climbs a wooded knoll to reach Hemenway Lookout, a ledge with a good winter view northward, at 3.39 m. The trail continues via a most unusual natural rock ramp (*Caution advised*), descends a ravine against the sheer rock face, then angles R onto another smaller ledge where it makes a very sharp R turn, climbs slightly, then descends abruptly to E. Chippens Hill Rd. (paved) at 3.7 m. (Black Dot Route, the Barnes Nature Center Connector, leads R (S), 2.84 m. to nature center on Shrub Rd., Bristol). At this point it turns L (N) to junction at 4.21 m. (Orange Dot Route leads straight ahead (N) and along E. Chippens Hill Rd.) The Mainline turns R up a bank onto the Sessions Woods Trail. Crossing two ridges as it skirts the edge of Sessions Woods Swamp, it gains higher ground at 4.7 m. Crossing this it descends and enters a pine plantation at 4.84 m., and shortly leads into a woodroad trace. It follows this through the plantation, turning squarely R at its edge onto another wood road from which it veers L shortly to regain the original route of the Sessions Wood Trail at 5.03 m. Thereafter the trail is gently rolling. It turns L onto a service road at 5.62 m., and reaches Rt. 69 at 5.71 m.

Trail continues L on Rt. 69 for 150 ft., then bears obliquely R across an intersection and enters a New Britain Watershed service road (barricaded). Whigville Brook is reached and crossed. Beyond the brook a good service road leads to Clark Corners at 6.41 m. (Orange Dot Route leads L to Rt. 69 at Lamson Corner in .77 m. and Pink Dot Route leads R to Devils Kitchen and Stone Rd. in 1.73 m.) The Mainline continues straight along the old road (Cornwall Rd.) and gradually climbs Scranton Mt. At 6.71 m. the trail leaves the old road bearing R along a tractor road and shortly reaching the foot of a steep slope. Bearing L it climbs the slope and gains another tractor road, bearing L. In 150 yds. in a cut-over area it leaves this road and passes through an old stone fence barway into the Nassahegon State Forest, named for a chief of the Tunxis tribe. At 7.12 m. it reaches a junction with the

Green Dot Route at Miller Rd., a forest service road. (Green Dot Route joins White Dot Route in .64 m.) The Mainline turns R along Miller Rd., leaving it at 7.21 m. to continue straight along an old wood road. This peters out soon and a footpath leads down a long hill, traverses a glacial esker, climbs over a sharp knob, turns sharply R, and at 7.86 m. arrives at Stone Rd. Jct., on another forest service road. (Pink Dot Route leads to Devil's Kitchen in .71 m.) The Mainline turns L and follows the service road about 700 ft. to Stone Rd., a passable gravel road at 8 m. (Red Dot Route continues straight leading over Wildcat and Taine Mts., to Perry's Lookout.) The Mainline turns L, (N) along Stone Rd. At 8.25 m., it turns sharply L, downgrade, along another service road. In .12 m. the trail veers L off this road and shortly reaches the George Washington Turnpike, here a narrow gravel road, at 8.65 m.

Here, the through hiker has a choice of route as the Mainline splits to form the Punch Brook Closed Circuit. The western side of this elongated loop measures 1.49 m.; the eastern, 1.65 m. Both offer a wide variety of hiking and are blazed in all blue without code dots.

PUNCH BROOK WEST

Punch Brook West turns L along this "turnpike" for about 100 yds., and then drops steeply into a valley on the R. Crossing a small seasonal brook it climbs gradually through open woods, crossing a wood road, to the saddle of a ridge. Turning R, it follows a horse trail briefly, veering L from it to drop steeply into a second valley where it crosses another forest road. Passing over a knoll, it then climbs a gentle ridge in pines, turning L near its summit to gain another horse trail in about 50 yds. Now bearing R it reaches Punch Brook Rd., at 9.12 m.

Punch Brook West now jogs R, downgrade, along Punch Brook Rd., for about 90 yds., bearing L into a wood road. Climbing gradually, the wood road peters out in about .12 m. but another is soon joined. This also terminates in about 175 yds., and the trail continues straight ahead through heavy laurel as a footpath. Emerging into a clearing, it joins discontinued service road at 9.52 m. This road descends a hill in a sweeping arc to the

R, terminating in a brushy clearing at 9.85 m. Punch Brook West now leads straight ahead into the woods (avoid horse trail leading R) and crosses a low hill to Hemlock Hill Jct., the northern terminus of the Punch Brook Closed Circuit at 10.14 m.

PUNCH BROOK EAST
(Mainline cumulative mileage continued.)

Punch Brook East makes a direct crossing of the narrow "turnpike," climbing a steep, sandy bank on its N side. It passes over a small hill and at 8.73 m. turns squarely R down a woodroad trace. In about 90 yds., the trail angles L to descend a minor ridge gaining a horse trail at 8.83 m. In about 125 yds., when the horse trail makes a pronounced turn L, Punch Brook East continues straight and descends to and crosses Punch Brook at 8.94 m. It now climbs briefly and bears L along another horse trail which it follows for the most part to Punch Brook Rd. which it crosses squarely at 9.14 m.

North of Punch Brook Rd., the trail passes through heavy ground hemlock, slabs a hillside through open field, and then gradually descends along the valley of Punch Brook to junction with Red Dot Route at 9.38 m. (Perry's Lookout, .71 m.). Continuing NE Punch Brook East crosses the brook on a footbridge at 9.45 m. A few yards beyond the bridge the trail turns very sharply L and makes a steep ascent of a glacial terrace. Turning L at its top, it skirts the edge of the terrace. It then descends a gully, crosses the mouth of another one, and reclimbs the terrace N. The way now leads across a plateau of oak followed by an open field and then through a fine pine grove, once the site of a baseball diamond!

Skunk Rock Rd. is diagonally crossed at 9.94 m. Now the trail follows the edge of a wooded marsh for nearly 500 ft., crossing its outlet along the top of an old stone wall. Bearing sharply L through hemlocks it shortly climbs a natural ramp up a ledge at 10.09 m., and after passing over a low hill through fine pine and hemlock forest, reaches Hemlock Hill Jct., northern terminus of the Punch Brook Closed Circuit, at 10.3 m.

THE MAINLINE (Continued)
(Cumulative mileage based on Punch Brook West. Add .16 m. for Punch Brook East.)

As a single route again the Mainline descends through beautiful hemlock forest. At 10.28 m. it turns squarely R along a wood road. (White Dot Route leads L, to George Washington Tnpke. .9 m.) The wood road is followed to Skunk Rock Rd. where the trail bears L, downgrade. After crossing the immediate valley of Bradley Brook to Rt. 4, it bears L along this highway. In 600 ft., a parking shoulder is reached at 10.68 m. (Burlington, 1.1 m. W.) To continue on the Tunxis, go W on Rt. 4. Take 2nd R at .94 m. (Covey Rd.) Again take 2nd R at 1.93 m. (Hotchkiss Rd.) Trailhead will be found (L) at 2.19 m.

THE WHITE DOT TRAIL

The White Dot route is the longest and westernmost color-coded route, and the first to diverge north from the Mainline. This trail provides a North/South connection for both the Main Line/Mile of Ledges Trail and the Yellow Dot Trail. It features beaver lodges and the summit of Johnnycake Mountain.

0.00 Trail begins at Old Marsh Jct., .8 mi. on the Main Line/Mile of Ledges Trail.

0.05 E. Church Road (paved) turn R (N).

0.41 R up a private driveway (Do not block). Then sharp L about 20 yards into woods. Trail climbs a long hill, crosses its top, and descends to one of the headwater branches of Poland River.

1.58 Emerge from woods and follow a Bristol Water Dept. service road.

1.74 Through gate and cross Blueberry Hill Road.

2.71 Pass through yard. A farther driveway is followed and then the route leads straight along an old wood road.

3.26 Turn sharp R onto old Polly Dan Road. Cross a swamp then turn L and climb a pronounced hill. Near the summit the trail bears R and becomes a shady lane between stone walls.

4.31 Reach Johnnycake Road (paved) and turn R (S).

4.69 Reach crest (Johnnycake Mountain (1150 ft.) is 100 yards L) and descend continuing on paved road.

5.01 The intersection with Old Field Road is the junction of the White Dot and Yellow Dot Trails. The Yellow dots begin straight ahead (S). The White Dots turn L (E) onto Old Field Road.

5.08 Turn L off Old Field Road onto a fence line wood road.

5.30 When the wood road bears left and up a grade, the trail now goes straight into woods and passes over and around several interesting rock outcropings.

5.56 Enter New Britain Watershed Property (posted).

5.73 Begin steep then gradual descent of the E slope of Johnnycake Mountain.

6.03 Cross tractor road after having crossed two small brooks. Then, after a short flat stretch begin final descent.

6.32 Cross an unusually high and wide stone wall.

6.36 Cross small brook and climb knoll then R.

6.46 Cross Route 69. Cross branch of Whigville Brook.

7.14 Swing R and on contour reach Cornwall Road.

7.27 Reach Cornwall Road. Straight across into woods and in a few yards, bear square L.

7.29 Green Dot Route junction. (Green Dot Route R (S) .64 m. to Mainline on Miller Road.)

8.14 Leaving an old orchard, reach George Washington Turnpike (here paved). Turn R and follow road, then bear into pine woods.

8.34 Nassahegon State Forest service road.

8.53 Bear R. Trail now utilizes pieces of other forest roads as well as footpath.

9.08 Trail ends at Mainline.

THE YELLOW DOT TRAIL

This trail provides a North/South connection for both the Main Line/Mile of Ledges Trail and the White Dot Trail. It features Tory Den and Bryda Ledge.

- 0.00 Trail begins at 1.4 mi. on the Mainline/Mile of Ledges Trail.
- 0.15 Tory Den — A comparatively small rock formation, actually a tunnel beneath a rock, it was used as a hideout in the Revolutionary times by Chippens Hill Tories when Patriots came visiting. It is backdropped by a large and jagged ledge.
- 0.18 Trail descends a short rock staircase.
- 0.43 Cross brook.
- 0.66 Ascend to top of ledge with limited winter views.
- 0.77 Steep descent then L.
- 1.09 Greer Road Junction. Yellow Dot continues L (N). Trail to Greer Road on R. Greer Road will connect with Main Line/Mile of Ledges Trail.
- 1.15 Attain Bryda Ledge with limited winter views.
- 1.20 Cross small brook and then onto old road. The road becomes very wet during the spring and after a rain.
- 1.34 Road ends but continue straight (N).
- 1.45 Pass old stone foundations on left and then cross a wood road running (E/W).
- 1.76 Pass abandoned barbed wire fence running (N/S).
- 1.90 Victory Birch — Pass under a bowed over birch tree with two large branches forming a V.
- 2.42 Pass through an old stone wall and then cross a small stone bridge.
- 2.69 Trail emerges from woods onto Johnnycake Road (unpaved). Turn L and follow road (N).
- 2.96 Trail Ends at intersection of Old Field Road. White Dot South continues straight (N). White Dot North turns R (E).

THE BARNES NATURE CENTER CONNECTOR

This lengthy access route (coded with black dots on blue) leads from the Harry C. Barnes Memorial Nature Center on Shrub Rd., Bristol, to the Mainline on E. Chippens Hill Rd., .31 m. E of Hemenway Lookout.

Beginning immediately behind the Barnes Nature Center, this trail leads N through low shrubs parallel to an open field. The field ends in about

350 ft., and the trail continues into rather dry and open woods along the edge of a valley terrace. In 85 yds., avoid nature trail leading downgrade, R.

The edge of the terrace is followed for .13 m. Then the trail descends slightly and enters thicker woods. At .31 m. it gains a woodroad trace which it follows for about 75 yds., and then descends, R, to the immediate bank of Negro Hill Brook (known locally as Falls Brook). This is the only trail of the Southern Division of the Tunxis to follow a large stream closely for any great distance.

At .54 m. the trail leads onto a boardwalk bridging springs in mud and a tributary stream, and 100 yds. farther two more are bridged. Now the trail leaves the brook, following a low ridge between it and a swamp. At .79 m. it climbs a rocky bank and reaches Main St., Whigville.

Here it jogs R (E) a few yds., crossing the brook on the highway bridge, and immediately turns L up the driveway of the Backes Power Equipment Co. (*No parking in this driveway or yard.*) It follows the driveway to its end and then crosses lawn to a footbridge leading back across the brook. Here it bears L across the bridge and climbs steeply up the wooded side of the brook's very narrow valley.

Reaching the top it skirts the edge of this steep slope along a fence line for 125 yds., and then turns squarely L, upgrade, into a field where it gains another fence line. This it follows, crossing out of the pasture over a stile to Rt. 69 at 1.05 m.

The Connector makes a direct crossing of Rt. 69 climbing a steep and sandy bank on its W side. Now it crosses the flattish top of a knoll through dry, open woods. At 1.16 m. the trail turns R and descends steeply to Negro Hill Brook which it again follows closely for a short distance. Bearing L, it climbs a minor ravine and shortly climbs steeply out of this to the R.

Traveling now W the Connector drops slightly and traverses open moist woods gaining a wood road trace which it follows into the entrance of Birch Valley. It leaves this trace to the R at 1.39 m.

For the next thousand feet the Connector climbs Birch Valley SW in a series of gentle windings culminated by a steep direct assault on the valley's headwall. Gaining a wood trace it descends somewhat W for about 90 yds., leaving the trace in a minor valley to continue straight ahead at 1.64 m.

The next 300 yds. offer a variety of going — ledge, dense thickets, a rock field, and the climb to a hillside shelf where the trail bears R into an old horse trail at 1.81 m. The Connector follows the horse trail NW about 150 yds., as the Great Wall, a nearly sheer rock escarpment 60 to 75 ft. high develops on the L. After passing some huge boulders the trail diverges L, from the horse trail and approaches the immediate base of the Great Wall which it follows R for another 70 yds. It then climbs a natural ramp of broken rock fragments, passing under an overhang, and reaches the top of the Great Wall through a crevice at 1.96 m.

Climbing a little more to the top of the ridge (winter view), the trail enters a section known as Ford's Boulevard where its route was cut through laurel. Passing over a sharp knoll, the Connector bears R and descends into the Avenue of the Ledges, a box ravine, at 2.09 m.

The passage down the Avenue is mostly rough footing although a woodroad trace is followed briefly. Bearing L the trail climbs out of the Avenue and gains another woodroad trace at 2.33 m.

Now there is a gradual climb (wet in spring) for about .2 m. and as the wood road bears L, the Connector goes straight through a grove of hemlock. At 2.51 m. it reaches a limited viewpoint overlooking Sessions Woods Swamp.

It now descends in a series of switchbacks along natural ramps through a hemlock-clad dell on the side of a ledgy escarpment to the floor of the swamp where it abruptly reverses direction (now SW) and leads up an arm of the swamp. In about 150 yds., it bears R and crosses a small stream. Shortly it reaches a woodroad trace which it follows briefly and then bears away from it (R), climbs over a ledge, and descends to another small stream. Beyond this stream it bears R again and angles into E. Chippens Hill Rd., in about 75 yds., reaching the Mainline at 2.84 m. (Hemenway Lookout, .31 m. L.)

THE ORANGE DOT ROUTE

This route leads from the western terminus of the Sessions Woods Trail via Lamson Corner to Clarks Corners.

Leaving the above-mentioned point it continues N on E. Chippens Hill Rd. At .51 m. as the gravel road bears sharply R, the trail continues straight down an old road. In about 400 ft. it crosses Whigville Brook and climbs briefly to Rt. 69 at .67 m., where Scoville Rd. enters from the W (Lamson Corner). The Orange Dots cross Rt. 69 here and enter the woods beside the Lamson Corner Cemetery along a New Britain Watershed service road that follows the route of the old Torrington Tnpke. Passing over gently rolling terrain this route terminates at Clarks Corners at 1.42 m. (Mainline runs R and L, the Pink Dot Route continues straight ahead.)

THE PINK DOT ROUTE

This route leads from Clarks Corners, a crossing of service roads on the New Britain Watershed, via Devils Kitchen to Stone Rd. Jct., 700 ft. W of Stone Rd. in the Nassahegon State Forest.

Leaving Clarks Corners eastward the Pink Dot Route goes along the service road that follows the route of the old Torrington Tnpke., over slightly rolling terrain. At .61 m., it bears L at the foot of a hill into a tractor road and in about 500 ft. bears L again to enter the box ravine known as Devils Kitchen. The deepest part of the ravine is reached at .88 m. Thereafter, the trail, having gained a plateau where maidenhair ferns abound, meanders across it and drops down its abrupt E side, then turns L along an old road. This is followed for about 600 ft. whereupon the trail passes over a very sharp knoll, then climbs slightly through a minor col and descends to a service road of the Nassahegon State Forest and Stone Rd. Jct., at 1.59 m. (Mainline continues straight ahead and also R.)

THE GREEN DOT ROUTE

This link between the Mainline and the White Dot Route leaves the former at Miller Rd., a Nassahegon State Forest service road, about 600 ft. E of Cornwall Rd. This link passes over three minor ledges before descending steeply to the White Dot Route at a point about 100 yds. E of Cornwall Rd. Limited NE view in winter from the northernmost ledge. However, it does cross a very large charcoal circle, and passes a large glacial erratic. Distance .64 m.

THE RED DOT ROUTE

This route leads from Stone Rd., in the Nassahegon State Forest over Wildcat and Taine Mts., to Punch Brook East, giving access to Perry's Lookout.

Leaving Stone Rd., the Red Dot Route climbs gradually for about 700 ft., then levels off until it slabs the N slope of Wildcat Mt. It now crosses a col to a minor knoll, then descends moderately to an outlook ledge at .68 m. It then descends the ledge steeply and turns L into an old road. At .76 m. it crosses Wildcat Brook. In another 50 yds. it bears L away from the road and travels through hemlocks high above the brook. At 1.03 m. it bears R near a private yard and passes beside a sharp knob to George Washington Tnpke. (here paved) at 1.13 m. Crossing this road it climbs toward the summit of Taine Mt. (900 ft.), utilizing an old road at first. This peak, with unusual strata in its ledges and a couple of glacial erratics, is reached at 1.78 m.

Descending slightly N for about 250 ft., the trail then climbs a steep bank. (Avoid old route leading R.) Then it gradually descends a broad ridge to a col (sometimes wet) at 2 m., and climbs onto a more pronounced and somewhat ledgy ridge, the high point of which is reached at 2.18 m. At the summit of this ridge the Taine Mt. Nature Conservancy Tract is entered. *Please do not disturb or injure plant, animal, or bird life.* Descending N, first along this ridge and then down its W side, Perry's Lookout is reached at 2.41 m. (Extensive western view.)

Bearing L the trail descends the S end of the ledge steeply and in about 600 ft. reaches a junction with an access route leading to Punch Brook and Taine Mt. Rds.

Bearing L at this junction the Red Dot Route descends gradually through moist but open woods, and then more steeply, crossing a brook at 2.7 m. It then climbs rather steeply to a glacial terrace and crosses Punch Brook Road (limited parking) at 2.84 m.

N of Punch Brook Rd., it descends gradually across an old gravel pit, bearing L at its N edge and then descends steeply R into a wood road trace. In a few yards it bears L on another trace which peters out and then as a footpath reaches Punch Brook East at 3.12 m.

An easier descent may be made from Perry's Lookout by leaving it to the N. Here a moderate slope is descended and Taine Mt. Rd. reached at 2.6 m. (paved). Bearing L (downgrade), Punch Brook Rd. is reached at 3.0 m.

HOTCHKISS ROAD, BURLINGTON TO U.S. 202

(U.S.G.S. quadrangle: Collinsville)

Between Hotchkiss Rd., Burlington and U.S. 202 in New Hartford, the Southern Tunxis is a continuous route. Most of the distance is on Nepaug Reservoir watershed.

This section of the Tunxis Trail leaves the NW side of Hotchkiss Rd., at a point almost opposite a tablet commemorating the Hotchkiss Watch Factory. Its foundations may be seen between the street and Bunnell Brook a short distance E. A few yds. into the woods the trail closely passes the foundations of the Hotchkiss residence. It crosses a gravel road at .23 m., goes around a white gate, and enters Hartford's Metropolitan Watershed via Smith Service Rd. At 1 m. the trail crosses Phelps Brook on a bridge, and 200 ft. farther leaves the service road R, and traverses sharply rolling country through heavy hardwoods with an undergrowth of young pine, hemlock and spruce. At 1.27 m. the trail emerges at the corner of Valentine and Douglas service roads. It continues straight (N) via Douglas. This road now climbs over Garrett Mt., passing just E of its 910 ft. peak at 2.06 m. and reaches Garrett Service Rd. at 2.75 m. Here it turns L, downgrade. Nepaug River Rd., another service road, is reached at 3.36 m. Turning L onto it the trail passes a cow pasture and leaves the road abruptly (R) along the pasture's western fence-line at 3.41 m. It now briefly leaves the fenceline to cross a small brook; then regains the fenceline and climbs gradually to Southeast Rd., (paved) at 3.63 m.

Turning R, the trail now follows Southeast Rd. (Spencer Rd. on Collinsville G.S. sheet) to a high tension line at 3.93 m. where it leaves the road, R. Angling across the high line, it enters a pine plantation and then later recrosses the high line to the immediate bank of the Nepaug River. Turning L, it reaches U.S. 202 at 4.16 m. Bearing R, the trail follows U.S. 202 for 800 ft. to the southern access road into the Nepaug State Forest. (This is the 2nd gravel road on the L.)

NEW HARTFORD — U.S. 202 TO RT. 44

(U.S.G.S. quadrangles: Collinsville, New Hartford)

This section of the Southern Tunxis has a mainline route, two loops, and a dead-end spur. It is not color-coded. N of U.S. 202 the Tunxis initially follows the southern access road into the Nepaug State Forest. In a little over 500 ft. it reaches a "T" intersection and continues slightly L, upgrade into open woods. Passing over a low rise it crosses a service road at .18 m., and then climbs steeply. Gaining a ridgeline, the trail swings L and follows it for several hundred feet, then descends a valley to the R through heavy hemlock. It emerges at a service road intersection at .54 m. Continuing straight through the intersection, it follows a service road to its intersection with Pine Hill Rd. at .82 m. Bearing R along Pine Hill Rd., it intersects with Satan's Kingdom Rd. at .93 m., and bears L along it. (Tipping Rock Loop enters L.) The Mainline continues N along Satan's Kingdom Rd. to junction at 1.28 m. (Shelter 4 Loop enters R). In about another 900 ft. Satan's Kingdom Rd. starts down a long hill near the foot of which there is a spring, L. At 2.05 m., trail reaches junction. (Shelter 4 Loop leads R along a passable gravel road.) The N end of the Tipping Rock Loop is reached at 2.31 m., and the Mainline, continuing straight ahead, follows Satan's Kingdom Rd. and veers R at 2.39 m., skirts the edge of Satan's Kingdom Gorge, then returns to Satan's Kingdom Rd. (here paved) at 2.72 m. and descends to Rt. 44 where it turns R and crosses the highway bridge at 2.91 m.

TIPPING ROCK LOOP

Leaving the intersection of Pine Hill and Satan's Kingdom Rds., the Tipping Rock Loop climbs through young pine and soon crosses a high tension line. It crosses several wood roads. Just short of the high point at 1.27 m., the Valley Outlook Trail branches L. Main trail now climbs steeply to the summit of Tipping Rock Ledge at 1.3 m., descends E steeply, then turns N (L). In a short distance it begins its gradual descent in a sweeping curve R. Part way down it picks up an old wood road and reaches Satan's Kingdom Rd. at 2.04 m.

VALLEY OUTLOOK TRAIL

This trail affords access to the otherwise trailless and roadless western section of the Nepaug State Forest. It is a deadend spur leading to a fine outlook.

Leaving the col just S of Tipping Rock, the trail crosses a small brook (undependable), then bears R, passing behind Tipping Rock. In about 500 ft. it scrambles up the steep S end of Queen Mary Ledge. (Limited views.) Turning W at the ledge it descends to a wood road and bears L. At a large white oak the trail turns sharply L. From this point it follows a rocky ridgeline, then passes over two knolls. Just beyond the summit of the second it passes through a fine grove of hemlock, then slabs a hillside. At .5 m., it reaches a large lone hemlock and bears L. It follows a definite ridge, passing over every knob, then bears R and crosses a wooded tableland with two prominent charcoal circles. At the SW edge of the tableland the trail bears L and shortly climbs steeply to the Rome Spare Outlook, a ledge with an extensive W view of Yellow Mt. and the Nepaug Valley at 1.17 m.

SHELTER FOUR LOOP

NOTE: The footway of the first half of this trail is in poor condition because of vehicle abuse.

This loop leaves Satan's Kingdom Rd., approx. .3 m. N of its intersection with Pine Hill Rd., and the S end of the Tipping Rock Loop. It descends steeply E along a woodroad trace for about 500 ft., turning L along Bampton Rd. This is followed gradually downgrade for about .65 m. Then the trail bears L, reversing its direction as it drops down by a little stream. Crossing this in a fine hemlock forest, it crosses an open knoll and descends through mature white pine to a forest service road. Turning L on this it reaches Satan's Kingdom Rd., in .2 mile at a point .25 m. S of the N end of the Tipping Rock Loop. (Total distance: .97 m.)

NEW HARTFORD, BARKHAMSTED, HARTLAND REGION

(U.S.G.S. quadrangles: Collinsville, New Hartford, West Granville, Mass.)

Between U.S. 44 at Satan's Kingdom and the Mass. line there are twenty miles of the most beautiful woodland trail that can be found in the state (See Tunxis map "Satan's Kingdom North"). From Satan's Kingdom Rd. the trail follows Rt. 44 bridge E across Farmington River. At end of bridge it goes L down embankment and along the river, over a brook, and across fields to Puddletown Rd. in .5 m. (Alternate route along U.S. 44 to Puddletown Rd. travels N on Puddletown Rd. for .5 m.) Trail then ascends steeply to the R (E) and stays in the woods, then goes through a recreation camp using Ratlum Brook, dammed up, as a swimming area and turns R about 50 feet after crossing the bridge; the trail proceeds back into the woods and reaches Ratlum Rd., New Hartford at 3.6 m. Go R (E) along the blacktop, around the sharp bend and pass Ski Sundown. At 4.2 m. trail goes L into the woods. Proceeding N over Ratlum Mt. the trail affords beautiful views of Compensating and Barkhamsted reservoirs. The trail reaches Ratlum Rd., Barkhamsted, crosses it and goes N through the Metropolitan District Commission property, crosses Rt. 219, then to Washington Hill Rd. and the old Bradley foundation. This is the site of the old clay pit which made the bricks for the community house at the intersection of Rts. 219 and 179. Progressing N, cross Kettle Brook to the top of "Injun" caves, not really caves but huge boulders used by the Indians as a gathering area. The trail continues N over Pine Mt. (1391 ft.), a site used for hawk watching during the migration period. Coming down from Pine Mt. cross Pine Mt. Rd. Continuing N across Roberts Brook and another brook the trail reaches old Rt. 20 about 1.3 m. directly W of East Hartland. There is a picnic spot just to the N, and a fine brook beyond. From Rt. 20, 1.5 m. NW of East Hartland, the trail climbs to and goes along a fine ridge with a descent to Hurricane Rd. Thence N in a valley and E up a brook near the Mass. line to the end of Tunxis Trail at Pell Rd.

WATERBURY AREA TRAILS

HANCOCK BROOK-LION HEAD TRAIL

(U.S.G.S. quadrangle: Waterbury)

The trail starts at the end of Sheffield St., Waterville just E of the bridge across Hancock Brook. Proceed along an old rd., passing a Blue Trail on the L. The old rd. parallels Hancock Brook for 1.4 m., and then makes an abrupt L turn through large hemlock and ascends to top of Lion Head. Continue along ridge in a southerly direction with many viewpoints and descend to above-mentioned Blue Trail and starting point. Round trip about 3 m. (Sheffield St. turns R off Thomaston Ave. (old Rt. 8) just past the Ville Theatre in Waterville center.) See map Mattatuck Trail.

JERICHO TRAIL

(U.S.G.S. quadrangles: Waterbury, Thomaston)

Trail begins on the N side of Echo Lake Rd., .75 m. W of Rt. 8 overpass and the Watertown Drive-in Theatre. (Whitestone Cliffs Trail begins .9 m. E). Trail climbs steeply to top of ridge, turns R (E) continuing to viewpoint, turns L (NW) to dirt rd. It crosses rd. and after short climb, reaches wide power line right-of-way. (If blazes are difficult to follow, cross powerline to woods, bear L to regain trail.) Care should be taken at the power line because of illegal and dangerous rifle shooting in line with trail. Trail crosses powerline, enters woods and continues to Jericho Brook at 2.2 m., following brook for a short distance and then crossing to make a turn to continue N. Trail climbs to higher ground to reach jct. with Mattatuck Trail at Crane Outlook at 3 m. The trail crosses several hills and ravines typical of the region. See map Mattatuck Trail.

WHITESTONE CLIFFS TRAIL

(U.S.G.S. quadrangle: Waterbury)

Trail begins on the E side of old iron bridge located at the jct. of Echo Lake Rd. and Thomaston Rd. (Old Rt. 8), near the Watertown Drive-in

Theatre in Waterville. The trail follows old trolley bed between river and rd. N for .5 m., turns R at viaducted cross hwy., and continues along brook bank ascending steep hill to trail jct. at 1 m. Trail turns L, crosses brook and reaches base of cliffs at 1.3 m., climbing steep side of Whitestone Cliffs to summit at 1.5 m. with outstanding views of Naugatuck Valley. Trail follows zigzag route along ridge and descends into woods at 1.9 m., gaining wood rd. and crossing brook at 2.2 m., and bears R to reach jct. at 2.3 m. Main trail turns R and follows wood rd. to Mt. Tobe Rd. at 2.5 m., then turns R into woods. Trail continues climbing to cross a scenic falls, completes loop at 1.2 m., and then descends to starting point on Thomaston Rd. (Old Rt. 8) at about 3.7 m. See map Mattatuck Trail.

JERICHO-WHITESTONE CONNECTOR

Yellow dot trail begins at Frost Bridge and continues under Rt. 8. Trail leaves rd. as a rock cairn signals R turn up side of power line and then joins Jericho Trail at approx. 2.5 m. (approx. 400 yds. from power line).

WESTWOODS AND STONY CREEK QUARRY PRESERVE TRAIL

(U.S.G.S. quadrangles: Guilford, Branford)

Westwoods, located less than a mile W of the Guilford Green consists of about 1000 acres of ledge, forest and marsh. Large sections of land are owned by the State of Connecticut, the Guilford Land Conservation Trust, and the Town of Guilford, with the remainder under private ownership.

The trails of the Stony Creek Quarry Preserve are on more than 350 acres of similar terrain owned by the Town of Branford and the Branford Land Trust, along with some privately owned property. A 50 acre area situated within the preserve is leased by the Town of Branford to the Stony Creek Granite Corporation. It contains an active quarry not open to hikers.

See map Westwoods and Stony Creek Quarry Preserve Trails and map Southern Section White Trail.

The two trail systems are connected by a single trail blazed with a green rectangle. It consists of 3.5 miles of mostly level terrain extending from Dunk Rock Rd. in Guilford to Flat Rock Rd. in Branford. All trails are blazed in the colors indicated in the blaze legend shown in the lower left-hand corner of the map. Circles indicate main N-S trails. Rectangles mark E-W trails. Crossover and alternate routes are identified by square blazes in the color of the trail(s) to which they lead. Exceptions to this marking system in Westwoods are as follows: green triangles on the Nature Trail; yellow triangles on the Bridle Trail; red diamonds on the Charles Hubbard Memorial Trail; and metal diamonds on the Silver Trail. On all trails a change of direction is marked by two blazes, one above and to the R or L of the other, indicating a turn to the R or L. Two identical blazes, one directly above the other, mark the end of a trail.

The main trails blazed with circles in both systems travel over varying terrain, with the alternate square blazed routes generally providing easier walking. The Yellow Circle Trail of Westwoods from the plank walk S to Lost Lake is the most challenging, recommended only to the energetic. Just S of the Rt. 146 RR bridge off Sachem's Head Rd. is the John Rodman Paul Memorial Trail which affords spectacular views of Great Harbor.

All trails at some time cross private land. Please respect landowners' rights and assure continued trail use by observing these rules: No fires; no litter; no camping; confine your walks to marked trails; do not cut trees or disturb other plants; *motorized vehicles are prohibited from all trails.*

ZOAR TRAIL

(U.S.G.S. quadrangle: Southbury)

Trail is in the Lower Paugussett State Forest, Newtown. Access: From Rt. 34, about 100 yds. W of the intersection with Rt. 111 in Stevenson, turn

N on Great Quarter Rd. This rd. ends in 1.25 m. at a turn-around with parking space. See map Kettletown St. Park, Zoar Trail, Paugussett Trail.

0.0 From parking area follow an old rd. parallel to Lake Zoar.
0.2 A short deviation to the R avoids eroded section of rd.
0.3 The remains of the Mahar Cottage (private property). The charred sides of the trees show that the cottage burned. Trail ascends gradually through mixed forest.
0.5 Turn R and descend steeply to lake. (Apparent sand pit on far shore is Jackson Cove, a recreation area for the town of Oxford.)
0.7 Trail leaves shore and ascends on an old rd. (Notice that this rd. like several others appears to continue into the lake. The Stevenson Dam was completed in about 1919 and flooded the valley and several rds.)
0.9 Reach 100 ft. above the lake and return to the shore on another old rd.
1.2 Pass small beach. (Here or in muddy cove beyond deer and raccoon tracks are often found.) Trail turns inland through hemlock forest.
1.6 (Side trail descends to R to waterfall, lake shore and picnic area in 0.1 m.) Trail continues across Prydden Brook.
1.7 Avoid old rd. to L and continue straight ahead through hemlock forest about 100 ft. above lake.
2.4 Turn L and ascend steeply. (Path ahead goes into Cedarhurst, a private community.)
2.8 Reach 300 ft. above lake and descend gradually through mixed hardwood forest.
3.0 Ascend small hill, cross rocky top and enter hemlock forest.
3.2 Bear L up small knoll and then R to descend. Turn R on old forest rd.
3.4 Turn L across Prydden Brook. (250 ft. above lake) Go up hill through heavy laurel.
3.7 Bear L through small sag and over rock pile to view overlooking Lake Zoar to the S. (440 ft. above lake). Descend gradually through mixed hardwoods.

4.0	Cross old woods rd. Climb steeply.
4.2	Reach rocky summit at 520 ft. above lake. Continue through laurel with gradual descent.
4.7	Cross seasonal brook and then larger stream.
5.0	Ascend hill through laurel and hardwoods to 490 ft. above lake and then descend.
5.3	Reach stone embankment for an old forest rd. Descend gradually, crossing several seasonal streams.
5.8	Join old forest rd. at forest boundry. Notice that another old rd. joining at this point has become a stream.
6.0	Reach Great Quarter Rd. and turn L.
6.5	Reach turn-around and parking at end of Great Quarter Rd.